Freedom of Assembly and Petition

Other Books in the Bill of Rights series:

The Bill of Rights

Freedom of Assembly and Petition

Robert Winters, Book Editor

GREENHAVEN PRESS

An imprint of Thomson Gale, a part of The Thomson Corporation

THOMSON
GALE

Detroit • New York • San Francisco • New Haven, Conn. • Waterville, Maine • London

Bonnie Szumski, *Publisher*
Helen Cothran, *Managing Editor*

© 2006 Thomson Gale, a part of The Thomson Corporation.

Thomson and Star logo are trademarks and Gale and Greenhaven Press are registered trademarks used herein under license.

For more information, contact:
Greenhaven Press
27500 Drake Rd.
Farmington Hills, MI 48331-3535
Or you can visit our Internet site at http://www.gale.com

LIBRARY OF CONGRESS CATALOGING-IN-PUBLICATION DATA

Freedom of assembly and petition / Robert Winters, book editor.
   p. cm. -- (Bill of Rights (San Diego, Calif.))
  Includes bibliographical references and index.
  0-7377-3544-9 (hardcover : alk. paper)
  1. Assembly, Right of--United States--History--Juvenile literature. 2. Assembly, Right of--United States--Juvenile literature. 3. Petition, Right of--United States--History--Juvenile literature. 4. Petition, Right of--United States--Juvenile literature. 5. Freedom of association--United States--History--Juvenile literature. 6. Freedom of association--United States--Juvenile literature. I. Winters, Robert, 1963–
  KF4778.F74 2007
  323.4'8--dc22
                             2006025365

Printed in the United States of America
10 9 8 7 6 5 4 3 2 1

Contents

Chapter 1: The Historical Development of the Right of Assembly and Petition

Chapter 2: The Supreme Court Defines the Rights of Assembly and Association

Foreword

> "*I cannot agree with those who think of the Bill of Rights as an 18th century straightjacket, unsuited for this age. . . . The evils it guards against are not only old, they are with us now, they exist today.*"
>
> *Hugo Black, associate justice of the U.S. Supreme Court, 1937–1971*

The Bill of Rights codifies the freedoms most essential to American democracy. Freedom of speech, freedom of religion, the right to bear arms, the right to a trial by a jury of one's peers, the right to be free from cruel and unusual punishment—these are just a few of the liberties that the Founding Fathers thought it necessary to spell out in the first ten amendments to the U.S. Constitution.

While the document itself is quite short (consisting of fewer than five hundred words), and while the liberties it protects often seem straightforward, the Bill of Rights has been a source of debate ever since its creation. Throughout American history, the rights the document protects have been tested and reinterpreted. Again and again, individuals perceiving violations of their rights have sought redress in the courts. The courts in turn have struggled to decipher the original intent of the founders as well as the need to accommodate changing societal norms and values.

The ultimate responsibility for addressing these claims has fallen to the U.S. Supreme Court. As the highest court in the nation, it is the Supreme Court's role to interpret the Constitution. The Court has considered numerous cases in which people have accused government of impinging on their rights.

In the process, the Court has established a body of case law and precedents that have, in a sense, defined the Bill of Rights. In doing so, the Court has often reversed itself and introduced new ideas and approaches that have altered the legal meaning of the rights contained in the Bill of Rights. As a general rule, the Court has erred on the side of caution, upholding and expanding the rights of individuals rather than restricting them.

An example of this trend is the definition of cruel and unusual punishment. The Eighth Amendment specifically states, "Excessive bail shall not be required, nor excessive fines imposed, nor cruel and unusual punishments inflicted." However, over the years the Court has had to grapple with defining what constitutes "cruel and unusual punishment." In colonial America, punishments for crimes included branding, the lopping off of ears, and whipping. Indeed, these punishments were considered lawful at the time the Bill of Rights was written. Obviously, none of these punishments are legal today. In order to justify outlawing certain types of punishment that are deemed repugnant by the majority of citizens, the Court has ruled that it must consider the prevailing opinion of the masses when making such decisions. In overturning the punishment of a man stripped of his citizenship, the Court stated in 1958 that it must rely on society's "evolving standards of decency" when determining what constitutes cruel and unusual punishment. Thus the definition of cruel and unusual is not frozen to include only the types of punishment that were illegal at the time of the framing of the Bill of Rights; specific modes of punishment can be rejected as society deems them unjust.

Another way that the Courts have interpreted the Bill of Rights to expand individual liberties is through the process of "incorporation." Prior to the passage of the Fourteenth Amendment, the Bill of Rights was thought to prevent only the federal government from infringing on the rights listed in the document. However, the Fourteenth Amendment, which was passed in the wake of the Civil War, includes the words, "... nor shall any state deprive any person of life, liberty, or property, without due process of law; nor deny to any person within its jurisdiction the equal protection of the laws." Citing this passage, the Court has ruled that many of the liberties contained in the Bill of Rights apply to state and local governments as well as the federal government. This process of incorporation laid the legal foundation for the civil rights movement—most specifically the 1954 *Brown v. Board of Education* ruling that put an end to legalized segregation.

As these examples reveal, the Bill of Rights is not static. It truly is a living document that is constantly being reinterpreted and redefined. The Bill of Rights series captures this vital aspect of one of America's most cherished founding texts. Each volume in the series focuses on one particular right protected in the Bill of Rights. Through the use of primary and secondary sources, the right's evolution is traced from colonial times to the present. Primary sources include landmark Supreme Court rulings, speeches by prominent experts, and editorials. Secondary sources include historical analyses, law journal articles, book excerpts, and magazine articles. Each book also includes several features to facilitate research, including a bibliography, an annotated table of contents, an annotated list of relevant Supreme Court cases, an introduction, and an index. These elements help to make the Bill of Rights series a fascinating and useful tool for examining the fundamental liberties of American democracy.

Introduction

In 1944, historian Arthur Schlesinger noted that "a country famed for being individualistic [is also] the world's greatest example of joiners." From the beginning, the same people who came to America to escape oppression or simply to start anew in a new land embraced the idea of thinking for oneself and succeeding through your own efforts. But most also embraced, or soon came to appreciate, the importance of working together in a new, unfamiliar, and often dangerous environment. Even as these colonies grew and prospered and ultimately found the strength to break away from England, these habits persisted. The reason, according to Alexis de Tocqueville in 1840, is that in a democracy "the citizens are independent and feeble; they can do hardly anything by themselves, and none of them can oblige his fellow men to lend him their assistance. They all, therefore, become powerless if they do not learn voluntarily to help one another."

De Tocqueville also noted a particular feature of American associations. In France, and throughout most of Europe, associations were often secretive and frankly subversive. People joined together to defy their rulers and sometimes to overthrow them. Their cause might be just or unjust, but their secrecy was based on the idea that government could not be convinced; it could only be resisted. For many Europeans, "private association" and "conspiracy" were interchangeable terms.

In the early American Republic, the situation was very nearly the opposite. Political parties and associations operated openly and actively sought converts. The idea that small groups of Americans had every right to present their case to the public at large became deeply engrained in the national character. From these grew the twin guarantees of the right to peaceable assembly and to petition for redress of grievances in the First Amendment.

A Bumpy Road

In theory, these rights extended to all. Even slaves had the right to petition the legislature for redress or for emancipation. And the founding generation could hardly pretend that association was only for those in fundamental agreement with the government. The American Revolution itself had grown out of the activities of the Committees of Correspondence, the Sons of Liberty, and the very illegal Continental Congress that adopted the Declaration of Independence. That declaration castigated George III's tyrannical response to the "repeated petitions" addressed to him "in the most humble terms."

In practice, of course, it has always been a little more complicated.

In the United States, it is not a question of challenging dictators or kings, but counteracting the tyranny of the majority. Despite an abstract belief in liberty, equality, and civil rights, the American majority has always been willing to tolerate or simply ignore injustices in its midst. Throughout much of American history, police had the power to break up groups of "loiterers," chase "undesirables" out of town, and in general to keep unpopular groups from bringing their message to a wider public.

A Boon for Unpopular Groups

But throughout the nineteenth century, a number of important issues ensured that the rights of assembly and petition would not be forgotten. First was the issue of abolishing slavery. Slavery made a number of people uncomfortable, but those who called for ending it outright were seen as dangerous radicals, especially those who believed in true racial equality. Nevertheless, they refused to be silenced, and in the 1840s they flooded Congress with so many petitions for outlawing slavery in the District of Columbia that representatives voted to refuse to accept any more such petitions. In the end of course, the abolitionists achieved their goal when Lincoln signed the Emancipation Proclamation and the Thirteenth Amendment banned slavery, while the Fifteenth granted blacks the right to vote.

This in turn prompted many women to question their own second-class status, and again some refused to do so quietly. Through mass demonstrations, White House picketing, parades, and hunger strikes, these women kept the issue before the nation, despite arrests and police violence. Finally, their efforts convinced a very reluctant President Woodrow Wilson to call for passage of a constitutional amendment to grant women the right to vote, which was finally ratified in 1920.

Even more powerful, in terms of sheer numbers and social impact, were the efforts of labor unions. Early on the labor movement realized that strikes were not enough. The unions also had to win over majority opinion, to counteract the obvious disruptive nature of labor disputes, and picketing was the means. Pickets ensured that the public understood that there were serious grievances behind the disputes, grievances that often affected all workers. These pickets were key to achieving many things we take for granted, such as the forty-hour workweek, overtime, and paid vacation.

De Jonge and the New Era

As with much of the Bill of Rights, the First Amendment right to assemble was seen as a restriction on the federal government, but not on state or local authorities. This meant that the Supreme Court largely stood aside on the question of balancing police powers with the right to organize on behalf of new or unpopular causes. This changed in 1937 with the case of *De Jonge v. Oregon.*

When the Communist Party organized a meeting in support of striking longshoremen in Portland, police invoked Oregon's criminal syndicalism act to break up the meeting and arrest one of the speakers, Dirk De Jonge. This rather vague act had been specifically designed to keep Communists from influencing the labor movement and police undoubtedly considered this a routine matter. The Supreme Court disagreed. Instead, it found for the first time that there was a fundamental right to freedom of assembly that neither local nor state governments could violate. By arresting and convicting De Jonge, whose only crime was addressing a meeting held by an unpopular political party, Oregon had violated his fundamental First Amendment rights, in the view of the Court.

Since then the Court has found a fundamental right to picket, a great boon to labor organizers, but no group benefited more from the Court's new standard than African Americans in the 1950s and 1960s. Throughout the struggle to repeal the Jim Crow laws that kept black people segregated and unequal, state governments in the South attempted to ban demonstrations, intimidate groups such as the NAACP [National Association for the Advancement of Colored People], and prevent the kind of sit-ins that were garnering support for the civil rights movement. The courts proved a vital ally in the struggle to bring the grievances of African Americans to the attention of the entire country. Similarly, the massive demonstrations launched by the anti-Vietnam War movement ultimately galvanized the wider public to call for an end to the war.

In turn, these movements revitalized the right to assembly itself. Today, the idea of taking to the streets to present your case is second nature to pro-life and pro-choice advocates, gay rights groups and antigay marriage forces. Even groups that seek to restrict civil rights, such as the Ku Klux Klan and the neo-Nazis, have managed to reinforce the fundamental right to peaceable assembly. One of the most traumatic and contentious cases in the history of the American Civil Liberties Union [ACLU] concerned the attempt by neo-Nazis to march in Skokie, Illinois, in 1977. Home to many Holocaust survivors, Skokie did everything it could to prevent the march. When the ACLU took the case on behalf of the Nazis, fighting it all the way to the Supreme Court, it lost many of its oldest and most loyal supporters. When it was all over, however, the absolute right of even the most unpopular groups to hold a public rally, even in the most emotionally charged setting, had been firmly and dramatically established.

The Future of an Old Right

As a new century dawned, it seemed that there were more ways than ever for groups to get their message out. The big three television networks have been joined by numerous cable news stations. Talk radio provides a platform for political partisans, with liberal Air America recently emerging to challenge the conservative giants like Rush Limbaugh and his various imitators. Anybody with Internet access can start a Web blog and attract like-minded readers, and some of these have grown quite popular and influential.

But it is just this sort of "niche effect" that makes the right of assembly more necessary. It is all too easy to retreat into a bubble of preconceptions and agreement, in which one's own opinions are simply reinforced by a particular media outlet and by the other members in a movement or a party or an ideology. To reach the other side, or even the unconvinced middle, it is necessary to enter the public square and challenge preconceptions. This may require overcoming age-old prejudices, threatening established institutions and authorities, and demanding that one's fellow citizens rethink assumptions they have taken for granted since childhood. At that point, as millions have discovered in the past, the constitutional right to peaceable assembly takes on a new urgency.

The Bill of Rights

CHAPTER 1

The Historical Development of the Right of Assembly and Petition

The Origins of the Right to Petition

Norman B. Smith

Although it is not currently one of the major issues that animate the courts or the people, securing the right to petition was a major victory in the attempt to hold governments accountable to their citizens. As Norman B. Smith reveals in the following excerpt, petitioning followed the growth of liberty in England. The Magna Carta guaranteed nobles the right to petition the crown in 1215. In 1628 the Petition of Right extended this absolute guarantee to Parliament, and in 1701 a group of jurors from the shire of Kent secured this right on behalf of all citizens. American colonists embraced the right to petition, extending it to the disenfranchised, including women, free blacks, and even slaves. Royal governors who tried to suppress petitions met with firm resistance and often faced disciplinary action from London for violating this acknowledged right. By the time of the American Revolution, petitioning was a popular and highly effective means of expressing the will of the people. The framers of the Constitution enshrined it in the First Amendment along with the freedoms of speech and religion.

A graduate of Harvard Law School, Smith is a practicing attorney, a constitutional scholar, and the author of American Constitutional Rights.

Petitioning, like most other contemporary human liberties, first arose as a practice in response to political needs of the time, later became regularized and institutionalized, and finally became a fixed right. The earliest petition recorded in our Anglo-American constitutional history is the English

Norman B. Smith, "Shall Make No Law Abridging: An Analysis of the Neglected, But Nearly Absolute, Right of Petition," *University of Cincinnati Law Review*, 1986. Copyright 2006 University of Cincinnati College of Law. Reproduced by permission.

leaders' petition in 1013 to [Anglo Saxon king] Aethelred the Unready. The king had fled to France during an invasion of the Danes, and the nobles' petition listed grievances and summoned Aethelred to appear in council. He responded by promising not to retaliate against them for setting forth their complaints and for the other actions they had taken, and by promising that he would remedy their grievances. These same two points—whether petitioners will be punished for their statements, and whether petitioners have the prerogative of instructing or commanding action of the government—have been the central features of the history of petitioning. Over the course of time, the former has been resolved in petitioners' favor, and the latter against them.

Magna Carta of 1215, the fundamental source of Anglo-American liberties, was the king's response to the barons' petition. This was one of several royal charters granted by Medieval English kings to guarantee baronial privileges and, to a lesser extent, popular rights. Petitioning as a right was specifically recognized in Magna Carta: "[I]f we [the king], our justiciar, or our bailiffs or any of our officers, shall in anything be at fault toward anyone, or shall have broken any one of the articles of the peace or of this security, and the offences be notified to four barons of the five-and-twenty, the said barons shall repair to us (or our justiciar, if we are out of the realm) and, laying the transgression before us, *petition to have the transgression redressed* without delay." The breakdown of feudalism and the emergence of a strong sovereign with a centralized bureaucracy during the reigns of Edwards I, II, and III [in the thirteenth and fourteenth centuries] provided the conditions under which petitioning developed its modern characteristics and in turn shaped the growth of the institutions of government that we know today.... Under Edward III, it became established practice at the opening of every session of parliament for the chancellor to declare the king's willingness to consider petitions of the people....

The Petition of Right

The Petition of Right of 1628 is reminiscent of Magna Carta; it resulted from a constitutional crisis and embodied personal rights that have become central to the Anglo-American system. Also, like Magna Carta, the Petition of Right contained a royal guarantee issued in response to a petition. At this point in English constitutional history, however, the struggle that initiated the petition was between parliament and the king rather than between the nobility and the king. The king had advised that he would never consent to a statute on the proposed terms of the Petition of Right. Parliament chose the "petition of right" as its vehicle to secure the desired guarantees because [as stated by G.B. Adams] the form "assumed the justice of the petitioner's case and went on the supposition that all that was necessary was to bring it to the king's attention and justice would at once be done." The king's answer did not agree to the demands, but it did recognize them as rights he was bound to uphold. The Petition of Right condemned certain abuses such as arbitrary imprisonment, forced billeting of troops, forced loans, and commissions of martial law.

During the era of the civil war and the interregnum in England [ca. 1640–1660], petitioning reached enormous popularity. In 1622, King James I issued a proclamation that granted "the Right of his subjects to make their immediate Addresses to him by Petition." His successor, Charles I, as late as 1644, invited any subjects with grievances to freely address themselves by petitions and promised that their complaints would be heard. John Pym's speech in the House of Commons in 1640 explained the constitutional necessity of frequent sessions of parliament for providing subjects with an opportunity to present their petitions. Petitions of unprecedented number and size, often accompanied by tumultuous crowds, were laid before parliament. . . .

In response to the number and size of petitions and the disorderly manner in which they were presented, in 1648 Parliament enacted an ordinance limiting the exercise of petitioning by allowing no more than 20 persons to present a petition to parliament and by requiring that the presentation be in a peaceful and orderly manner. The ordinance reflected that there had been tumultuous assemblies in connection with drawing up petitions, that petitions had been presented in a riotous manner, and that there had been bloodshed and danger to the government. However, this ordinance also was the first statute of England to recognize petitioning as a fundamental right: "[I]t is the Right and Privilege of the Subjects of England, to present unto the Parliament their just Grievances, by Way of Petition, in a due Manner; and they shall be always ready to receive such Petitions...."

The essential features of the ordinance of 1648 were reenacted in 1661, as the Act 13 Car. II, Stat. I, c. 5, which is still on the statute books of Great Britain. This statute made it an offense to obtain more than 20 signatures to a petition addressed to either king or parliament for any alteration in the church or state, unless with sanction of three county justices of the peace or a majority of the grand jury at assizes or at quarter session or, if from London, with approval of the Lord Mayor, aldermen, and common councilors. In any event, no petition was to be presented by more than ten persons. While this statute did not contain an express statement of the right to petition as set forth in the ordinance of 1648, its enumeration of limitations implies the existence of the right itself. Although the statute was passed in reaction to the extensive popular demonstrations that occurred during the civil war and interregnum, the fact that parliament curbed only the manner of petitioning and not the contents of the petitions also supports the conclusion that a right of petition had emerged....

The Kentish Petitioners

[Historian Frederic William] Maitland reports that in 1701 the grand jury of Kent presented a respectfully worded petition to the House of Commons, begging that the king be granted money urgently needed for prosecuting war against France. The house voted the petition scandalous and committed the petitioners to prison. From this account, it would seem that the right of petitioning . . . was merely a nominal right and not a right in practice. However, upon closer inquiry we learn that the case of the Kentish petitioners ultimately confirmed and secured the unfettered right of petition to the people of England for all time.

The Kentish petitioners had followed to the letter the Act of 13 Car. II., Stat. I, c. 5. Although the petition was such a popular statement that it was subscribed with many more signatures than the 20 allowed by the statute, it came within the statutory exception as having been sanctioned by justices of the peace or the grand jury. Five petitioners presented it to the house, exactly half the maximum allowed by the statute. The Kentish petition was delivered to parliament on May 8, 1701. The House of Commons reacted wrathfully. . . . The petitioners were given an opportunity to recant, which they refused to do, relying on their "right to petition this honourable House, according to the Statute of 13 Car. II." After a five-hour debate on May 9, the House voted the mildly and respectfully worded petition "scandalous, insolent and seditious," and ordered the petitioners committed.

Defoe's Attack

Daniel Defoe's [author of *Robinson Crusoe*] courageous and resourceful action of May 14, 1701 led to the vindication of the right to petition. He wrote and delivered to the House of Commons a remarkable tract entitled "Legion's Memorial," in which he defended the right to petition and protested against the imprisonment of the Kentish petitioners. Defoe was as scrupulous to violate the Act of 13 Car. II, Stat. I, c. 5, as the Kentish petitioners were to obey this law. He claimed to act on behalf of two hundred thousand, not the statutory maximum of 20: "Our name is Legion, and we are Many." He delivered it in the company of 16 armed men, defying the statutory limit of ten presenters. In contrast to the deferential tone of the Kentish petition, "Legion's Memorial" was vitriolic. Defoe's tract repeatedly accused Parliament of acting illegally, told the House it had been "ridiculous and impertinent" to vote the Kentish petition insolent, and condemned the House as dishonorable, oppressive, neglectful of its duty, and "scandalously vicious." . . .

Parliament retreated in the face of Defoe's attack. . . . Parliament was prorogued on June 23, 1701. The prorogation resulted in the release of the Kentish petitioners without further proceedings against them. Upon their release, the petitioners were greeted with tremendous public acclaim. . . .

The Right of Assembly

By the time of the American Revolution, petitioning had become extremely popular in England; it was no longer checked or penalized and was frequently successful. Indeed, it seems that petitioning, which by now had become an unqualified right, helped to nurture the yet unrecognized rights of press and assembly. . . . We shall see that public meetings widely developed as the means for preparing and subscribing to petitions. . . .

What develops as an accepted or even tolerated practice often is transmuted into a right. Such appears to have been the case with public assembly, and petitioning likely was the activity that brought about the practice of publicly assembling. In the eighteenth century, the right of public meeting was not yet an envisaged constitutional right. The law did not guarantee public assembly, but did not interfere with it either, unless a riot or rebellion came about. Preparation of petitions often required public meetings. As petitioning became more frequent in the latter part of the eighteenth century, public meetings likewise became more common.

Petitioning in the American Colonies

The experience with petitioning, speech, press, and assembly in colonial America was somewhat different from that in England. Some of the American immigrants were political dissidents who came to the New World to escape the Old World restrictions on expression. England did not have the ability to impose firm and consistent political control on the colonies because America was so distant. Also, political habits and attitudes differed greatly among the several colonies. At least in some parts of America, these circumstances led to the toleration of a greater liberty of expression than was enjoyed in England, but also created some aberrational limitations on the right to petition that would have been unacceptable in contemporary England.

Chronologically, the adoption of the Body of Liberties by the Massachusetts Bay Colony Assembly in 1642 was the first significant event touching upon the rights of expression in America. During this time, according to [English historian Thomas] Macaulay, the liberties of the English nation were in their greatest peril, and "many looked to the American wilderness as the only asylum in which they could enjoy civil and spiritual freedom." In Massachusetts, people were concerned about the lack of a legal code and the exercise of excessive discretion by the magistrates. Governor [John] Winthrop appointed men to "frame a body or ground of laws in resemblance to a *magna charta*, which . . . should be received for fundamental laws." A proposed code was drafted, sent to the town meetings for their views, and adopted by the General Court. The resulting body of 100 laws codified for the first time in any legal system the right to petition:

[E]very man whether Inhabitant or Foreigner, free or not free, shall have liberty to come to any public Court, Council or Town meeting, and either by speech or writing, to move any lawful, seasonable or material Question, or to present any necessary Motion, Complaint, Petition, Bill or Information, whereof that Meeting hath proper cognizance, for it be done in convenient time, due Order and respective Manner.....

An excellent record of petitioning in colonial Virginia has been reconstructed. In Virginia, unlike New York, every effort to place limitations on the right to petition was successfully challenged. Petitioning became a vital part of the legislative process in eighteenth-century Virginia. More than half of all statutes that were enacted originated in the form of popular petitions, and the number of petitions per session more than doubled during the second half of the century. The celebrated "Ten Thousand Petition" seeking disestablishment of state religion was accompanied by 125 pages of signatures. The disenfranchised, including women, free blacks, and even slaves, were allowed to petition. The Virginia assembly, through two formal statements (1642 and 1664) on record, declared its primary purpose was for redress of grievances. Petitions on highly controversial topics were read in the assembly. The assembly deemed that it possessed the right to reject petitions worded in an insulting or obnoxious way, but there is no evidence that the assembly ever punished petitioners.

Governors Forced to Accept Right to Petition

Three colonial governors were thwarted in their efforts to interfere with the petitioning process. Governor Beckley received many petitions during the Indian War of 1675 requesting that he appoint a commander and undertake an active campaign against the Indians. He issued a proclamation forbidding further petitioning to the governor on that subject; complaints were made against the governor for the action, and the British government sent an investigatory commission. Governor Effingham became very angry over petitions complaining of unauthorized fees being charged by some officers; he threatened petitioners and demanded all petitions be given directly to him instead of to the legislature. The assembly refused to comply, sent an agent to England to protest his conduct in this and other matters, and secured his recall. Governor Spotswood, in contravention of a law passed in 1705 eliminating any discretionary powers the county judges may have had not to certify petitions they deemed improper, issued a proclamation in 1715 instructing county courts to refuse to certify "scandalous and seditious" petitions. The assembly ordered the judges to appear before the house, declaring their action to have been "Arbitrary and Illegal and a Subverting of the Rights and Libertys of the People . . ." and proceeded to act upon uncertified petitions. By the late seventeenth century, the assemblies of Virginia, New York, Pennsylvania, and Maryland had established committees to deal with the increasing number of petitions. In the years preceding the Revolution, as the concept of popular sovereignty gained acceptance, petitioning activity dramatically increased. As the Revolution approached, the colonial assemblies themselves engaged in vigorous petitioning campaigns directed both to parliament and to the king. The assemblies protested the Stamp Act, Molasses Act, and other laws affecting the colonies. At least two of these petitions drew punitive responses, but the mother country imposed these sanctions against the colony or its officers, not against any person in his individual capacity.

The Declaration of Independence, which accused the king of trampling upon many liberties of the colonists, did not claim that petitioning itself had been punished, only that the petitions had not met with favorable response: "In every state of these Oppressions we have Petitioned for Redress in the most humble terms: Our repeated petitions have been answered only by repeated injury."

Express Affirmations

The right of petitioning in America was expressly affirmed in both pre-Revolutionary declarations and pre-union state constitutions. The Stamp Act Congress of 1765 set forth in its Declaration of Rights and Grievances that "it is the right of the British subjects in these colonies to petition the King or either House of Parliament." In 1774, the Declaration and Resolves of the First Continental Congress stated that the colonists "have a right peaceably to assemble, consider of their grievances, and petition the King; and that all prosecutions, prohibitory proclamations, and commitments for the same, are illegal." Declarations of rights by state conventions, including Pennsylvania (1776), Delaware (1776), North Carolina (1776), Vermont (1777), expressly included the right to petition. Massachusetts (1780), and New Hampshire (1783), except for North Carolina, Pennsylvania, and Vermont, which included no restrictions whatever upon the right to petition, these declarations qualified the right by specifying that it must be exercised in an "orderly and peaceable manner."

In their ratifying conventions for the proposed federal constitution, four of the American republics, Maryland, New York, North Carolina, and Virginia, specified that the right of petition should be guaranteed. Of these, only Maryland included the requirement of "peaceable and orderly manner." . . .

[Founding Father James] Madison drafted the provision of the First Amendment guaranteeing the right to petition. The House of Representatives debated extensively over the provision, and the Senate amended the language to its present form. The original proposed text of the First Amendment provided that "[t]he freedom of speech and of the press, and the right of the people peaceably to assemble and consult for their common good, and to apply to the Government for redress of grievances, shall not be infringed." Congressman Sedgwick moved to strike out "assemble and" because that was encompassed within the concept of free speech. Opponents of the motion stated that all the enumerated rights were separate rights inherent in the people and should be specifically protected against infringement by the government. The motion to strike was defeated.

Congress debated and rejected a motion to require representatives to submit to instructions of the electorate. Congress generally agreed, however, that popular opinion should be received and considered, and that the right to petition for redress of grievances must be respected. This action amounted to a formal acceptance of the tacit understanding that petitioners can command the government's reception of, but not its acquiescence in, their petitions.

The Senate rewrote the petition language to essentially its present form; after insignificant amendments in both House and Senate, it emerged in its present form: "Congress shall make no law ... abridging ... the right of the people ... to petition the government for a redress of grievances." ...

The Purposes of Petitioning

The purposes of the right to petition and the interests it serves can be garnered from its history:

1. Petitioning is the means by which peoples' problems that need governmental response are brought to the attention of the government.

2. Petitioning is a principal source of the government's information on popular attitudes concerning the way it has conducted public business.

3. Petitions often disclose and consequently remedy incompetence, corruption, waste and other government misconduct.

4. In a popular sovereignty, petitions can measure the degree of public approval enjoyed by the incumbent government and its prospects for being kept in office.

5. The right of petitioning is commonly of such great value that (a) disregard of this right has provoked popular uprisings, and (b) efforts to place "time, place, and manner" restraints upon it have been unsuccessful.

6. Extensive petitioning activity preceded a number of popular constitutional reforms, the most important of which was popular sovereignty.

7. The availability of petitioning as a popular right allows public feelings to be expressed in a peaceful, orderly way and may be a foil to revolution.

8. Petitioning, in a sense, is the fountain of liberties, because historically it was the first popular right to be recognized. Vigorous exercise of the right to petition has been associated with forward strides in the development of speech, press, and assembly. Conversely, when petitioning has been attacked ... the other expressive freedoms likewise have been suppressed.

Petitioning is a distinct right. It is independent of, and not subsumed under, freedom of speech and press. The state of affairs in eighteenth-century England manifest that petitioning was in practice an absolute right while speech and press were the constant subjects of seditious libel prosecutions and other restraints. Also, although freedom of assembly may owe much of its development to petitioning, these two rights are separable. Thus, public order regulations concerning meetings for framing and signing petitions and meetings for presentation of petitions to the government do not infringe upon the right to petition itself.

The Role of Associations in Early America

Alexis de Tocqueville

In 1831 French aristocrat Alexis de Tocqueville took a tour of the young United States, which he recounted in Democracy in America, *published in two volumes in 1835 and 1840. De Tocqueville met with many prominent Americans, such as President Andrew Jackson, but he also spent a great deal of time observing average Americans in a wide variety of settings, including the many private associations that flourished in the country. In the following excerpt, he describes the ease with which Americans form associations, the role of such associations in checking the tyranny of the majority, and the ways associations mirror American political ideals. He contrasts American associations, which were open and peaceful, with the secret societies and militant organizations in Europe, which undermined society and often proved more tyrannical than the governments they claimed to oppose.*

Despite his aristocratic birth and his father's strongly monarchist views, de Tocqueville emerged as a leading voice for democracy in France's Chamber of Deputies, to which he was elected in 1839, and helped write the constitution of France's Second Republic in 1848. Nevertheless, he maintained a healthy skepticism toward all government, and he consistently advocated strengthening charitable organizations and other private associations as a healthy counterweight to government power.

Democracy in America *has provided generations of historians and political scientists with an unusually insightful and wide-ranging examination of the ways early Americans put the ideals of their Constitution into practice.*

Alexis de Tocqueville, *Democracy in America*, Volume I. Translated by Henry Reeve. New York: D. Appleton & Company, 1904.

In no country in the world has the principle of association been more successfully used, or more unsparingly applied to a multitude of different objects, than in America. Besides the permanent associations which are established by law under the names of townships, cities, and counties, a vast number of others are formed and maintained by the agency of private individuals.

The citizen of the United States is taught from his earliest infancy to rely upon his own exertions in order to resist the evils and the difficulties of life; he looks upon social authority with an eye of mistrust and anxiety, and he only claims its assistance when he is quite unable to shift without it. This habit may even be traced in the schools of the rising generation, where the children in their games are wont to submit to rules which they have themselves established, and to punish misdemeanours which they have themselves defined. The same spirit pervades every act of social life. If a stoppage occurs in a thoroughfare, and the circulation of the public is hindered, the neighbours immediately constitute a deliberative body; and this extemporaneous assembly gives rise to an executive power which remedies the inconvenience before anybody has thought of recurring to an authority superior to that of the persons immediately concerned. If the public pleasures are concerned, an association is formed to provide for the splendour and the regularity of the entertainment. Societies are formed to resist enemies which are exclusively of a moral nature, and to diminish the vice of intemperance: in the United States associations are established to promote public order, commerce, industry, morality, and religion; for there is no end which the human will, seconded by the collective exertions of individuals, despairs of attaining.

Hereafter I shall have occasion to show the effects of association upon the course of society, and I must confine myself for the present to the political world. When once the right of association is recognised, the citizens may employ it in several different ways.

Defining Associations

An association consists simply in the public assent which a number of individuals give to certain doctrines, and in the engagement which they contract to promote the spread of those doctrines by their exertions. The right of association with these views is very analogous to the liberty of unlicensed writing; but societies thus formed possess more authority than the press. When an opinion is represented by a society, it necessarily assumes a more exact and explicit form. It numbers its partisans, and compromises their welfare in its cause: they, on the other hand, become acquainted with each other, and their zeal is increased by their number. An association unites the efforts of minds which have a tendency to diverge in one single channel, and urges them vigorously toward one single end which it points out.

The second degree in the right of association is the power of meeting. When an association is allowed to establish centres of action at certain important points in the country, its activity is increased and its influence extended. Men have the opportunity of seeing each other; means of execution are more readily combined, and opinions are maintained with a degree of warmth and energy which written language cannot approach.

Lastly, in the exercise of the right of political association, there is a third degree: the partisans of an opinion may unite in electoral bodies, and choose delegates to represent them in a central assembly. This is, properly speaking, the application of the representative system to a party.

Thus, in the first instance, a society is formed between individuals professing the same opinion, and the tie which keeps it together is of a purely intellectual nature; in the second case, small assemblies are formed which only represent a fraction of the party. Lastly, in the third case, they constitute a separate nation in the midst of the nation, a government within the Government. Their delegates, like the real delegates of the majority, represent the entire collective force of their party; and they enjoy a certain degree of that national dignity and great influence which belong to the chosen representatives of the people. It is true that they have not the right of making the laws, but they have the power of attacking those which are in being, and of drawing up beforehand those which they may afterward cause to be adopted.

Danger of Free Association in Some Regions

If, in a people which is imperfectly accustomed to the exercise of freedom, or which is exposed to violent political passions, a deliberating minority, which confines itself to the contemplation of future laws, be placed in juxtaposition to the legislative majority, I cannot but believe that public tranquility incurs very great risks in that nation. There is doubtless a very wide difference between proving that one law is in itself better than another and proving that the former ought to be substituted for the latter. But the imagination of the populace is very apt to overlook this difference, which is so apparent to the minds of thinking men. It sometimes happens that a nation is divided into two nearly equal parties, each of which affects to represent the majority. If, in immediate contiguity to the directing power, another power be established, which exercises almost as much moral authority as the former, it is not to be believed that it will long be content to speak without acting; or that it will always be restrained by the abstract consideration of the nature of associations which are meant to direct but not to enforce opinions, to suggest but not to make the laws.

The more we consider the independence of the press in its principal consequences, the more are we convinced that it is the chief and, so to speak, the constitutive element of freedom in the modern world. A nation which is determined to remain free is therefore right in demanding the unrestrained exercise of this independence. But the unrestrained liberty of political association cannot be entirely assimilated to the liberty of the press. The one is at the same time less necessary and more dangerous than the other. A nation may confine it within certain limits without forfeiting any part of its self-control; and it may sometimes be obliged to do so in order to maintain its own authority.

In America the liberty of association for political purposes is unbounded. . . .

The Necessity of Associations in America

It must be acknowledged that the unrestrained liberty of political association has not hitherto produced, in the United States, those fatal consequences which might perhaps be expected from it elsewhere. The right of association was imported from England, and it has always existed in America; so that the exercise of this privilege is now amalgamated with the manners and customs of the people. At the present time the liberty of association is become a necessary guarantee against the tyranny of the majority. In the United States, as soon as a party is become preponderant, all public authority passes under its control; its private supporters occupy all the places, and have all the force of the administration at their disposal. As the most distinguished partisans of the other side of the question are unable to surmount the obstacles which exclude them from power, they require some means of establishing themselves upon their own basis, and of opposing the moral authority of the minority to the physical power which domineers over it. Thus a dangerous expedient is used to obviate a still more formidable danger.

The omnipotence of the majority appears to me to present such extreme perils to the American republics that the dangerous measure which is used to repress it seems to be more advantageous than prejudicial. . . . There are no countries in which associations are more needed, to prevent the despotism of faction or the arbitrary power of a prince, than those which are democratically constituted. In aristocratic nations the body of the nobles and the more opulent part of the community are in themselves natural associations, which act as checks upon the abuses of power. In countries in which these associations do not exist, if private individuals are unable to create an artificial and a temporary substitute for them, I can imagine no permanent protection against the most galling tyranny; and a great people may be oppressed by a small faction, or by a single individual, with impunity. . . .

It cannot be denied that the unrestrained liberty of association for political purposes is the privilege which a people is longest in learning how to exercise. If it does not throw the nation into anarchy, it perpetually augments the chances of that calamity. On one point, however, this perilous liberty offers a security against dangers of another kind; in countries where associations are free, secret societies are unknown. In America there are numerous factions, but no conspiracies. . . .

American vs. European Associations

The greater part of Europeans look upon an association as a weapon which is to be hastily fashioned, and immediately tried in the conflict. A society is formed for discussion; but the idea of impending action prevails in the minds of those who constitute it: it is, in fact, an army; and the time given to parley serves to reckon up the strength and to animate the courage of the host, after which they direct their march against the enemy. Resources which lie within the bounds of the law may suggest themselves to the persons who compose it as means, but never as the only means, of success.

Such, however, is not the manner in which the right of association is understood in the United States. In America the citizens who form the minority associate, in order, in the first place, to show their numerical strength, and so to diminish the moral authority of the majority; and, in the second place, to stimulate competition, and to discover those arguments which are most fitted to act upon the majority; for they always entertain hopes of drawing over their opponents to their own side, and of afterward disposing of the supreme power in their name. Political associations in the United States are therefore peaceable in their intentions, and strictly legal in the means which they employ; and they assert with perfect truth that they only aim at success by lawful expedients.

The difference which exists between the Americans and ourselves depends on several causes. In Europe there are numerous parties so diametrically opposed to the majority that they can never hope to acquire its support, and at the same time they think that they are sufficiently strong in themselves to struggle and to defend their cause. When a party of this kind forms an association, its object is, not to conquer, but to fight. In America the individuals who hold opinions very much opposed to those of the majority are no sort of impediment to its power, and all other parties hope to win it over to their own principles in the end. The exercise of the right of association becomes dangerous in proportion to the impossibility which excludes great parties from acquiring the majority. In a country like the United States, in which the differences of opinion are mere differences of hue, the right of association may remain unrestrained without evil consequences. The inexperience of many of the European nations in the enjoyment of liberty leads them only to look upon the liberty of association as a right of attacking the Government. The first notion which presents itself to a party, as well as to an individual, when it has acquired a consciousness of its own strength, is that of violence: the notion of persuasion arises at a later period and is only derived from experience. The English, who are divided into parties which differ most essentially from each other, rarely abuse the right of association, because they have long been accustomed to exercise it. In France the passion for war is so intense that there is no undertaking so mad, or so injurious to the welfare of the State, that a man does not consider himself honoured in defending it, at the risk of his life.

Effect of Universal Suffrage

But perhaps the most powerful of the causes which tend to mitigate the excesses of political association in the United States is universal suffrage. In countries in which universal suffrage exists the majority is never doubtful, because neither party can pretend to represent that portion of the community which has not voted. The associations which are formed are aware, as well as the nation at large, that they do not represent the majority: this is, indeed, a condition inseparable from their existence; for if they did represent the preponderating power, they would change the law instead of soliciting its reform. The consequence of this is that the moral influence of the Government which they attack is very much increased, and their own power is very much enfeebled.

In Europe there are few associations which do not affect to represent the majority, or which do not believe that they represent it. This conviction or this pretension tends to augment their force amazingly, and contributes no less to legalize their measures. Violence may seem to be excusable in defence of the cause of oppressed right. Thus it is, in the vast labyrinth of human laws, that extreme liberty sometimes corrects the abuses of license, and that extreme democracy obviates the dangers of democratic government. In Europe, associations consider themselves, in some degree, as the legislative and executive councils of the people, which is unable to speak for itself. In America, where they only represent a minority of the nation, they argue and they petition.

How Associations Are Governed

The means which the associations of Europe employ are in accordance with the end which they propose to obtain. As the principal aim of these bodies is to act, and not to debate, to fight rather than to persuade, they are naturally led to adopt a form of organization which differs from the ordinary customs of civil bodies, and which assumes the habits and the maxims of military life. They centralize the direction of their resources as much as possible, and they intrust the power of the whole party to a very small number of leaders.

The members of these associations respond to a watchword, like soldiers on duty; they profess the doctrine of passive obedience; say rather, that in uniting together they at once abjure the exercise of their own judgment and free will; and the tyrannical control which these societies exercise is often far more insupportable than the authority possessed over society by the government which they attack. Their moral force is much diminished by these excesses, and they lose the powerful interest which is always excited by a struggle between oppressors and the oppressed. The man who in given cases consents to obey his fellows with servility, and who submits his activity and even his opinions to their control, can have no claim to rank as a free citizen.

The Americans have also established certain forms of government which are applied to their associations, but these are invariably borrowed from the forms of the civil administration. The independence of each individual is formally recognised; the tendency of the members of the association points, as it does in the body of the community, toward the same end, but they are not obliged to follow the same track. No one abjures the exercise of his reason and his free will; but every one exerts that reason and that will for the benefit of a common undertaking.

CHAPTER 2

The Bill of Rights

The Supreme Court Defines the Rights of Assembly and Association

The Right of Assembly
Is Fundamental

Charles Evans Hughes

The United States had its first wave of anti-Communist hysteria in the 1920s, and a number of states passed laws against "criminal syndicalism," aimed primarily at keeping Communists from organizing workers or infiltrating the labor movement. Although defined somewhat differently in various states, criminal syndicalism generally involves advocating violence, sabotage, or other illegal acts for the purpose of overthrowing government or capitalist institutions. In July 1934, in the midst of the Great Depression, Dirk De Jonge addressed a meeting in Portland, Oregon, sponsored by the Communist Party to protest the shooting of longshoremen during a strike and the common police practice of raiding labor halls. Police raided the meeting and arrested De Jonge, who was duly convicted for violating Oregon's criminal syndicalism statute and sentenced to seven years in prison. He appealed, and in 1936 the case of De Jonge v. State of Oregon *came before the U.S. Supreme Court.*

The Court had two questions to consider. The first was whether De Jonge's right to peaceable assembly had been violated without justification. In the majority opinion, excerpted here, Chief Justice Charles Evans Hughes answered in the affirmative. He notes that De Jonge was convicted merely for participation in a public meeting without regard to the content of that meeting or his particular words or actions. Second, the Court had to determine whether the right to assemble was constitutionally protected against infringements by state governments as well as the federal government. By finding that Oregon had violated De Jonge's due process rights under the Fourteenth Amendment, the Court held that the right to assembly was inviolable

Charles Evans Hughes, majority opinion, *De Jonge v. State of Oregon*, 299 U.S. 353, January 4, 1937.

without strong justification. Indeed, Hughes writes that it is as fundamental as freedom of speech and of the press. Therefore, he includes it as one of the rights against both state and federal action.

Hughes had a distinguished public career as governor of New York, U.S. secretary of state, and a judge on the Permanent Court of International Justice, established by the League of Nations. He was first appointed to the Supreme Court in 1910 but resigned in 1916 to run for president against Woodrow Wilson. In 1930 he was reappointed, this time as chief justice, by President Herbert Hoover, and served in that capacity until his resignation in 1941.

Appellant, Dirk De Jonge, was indicted in Multnomah County, Or., for violation of the Criminal Syndicalism Law of that State. The act . . . defines "criminal syndicalism" as "the doctrine which advocates crime, physical violence, sabotage, or any unlawful acts or methods as a means of accomplishing or effecting industrial or political change or revolution". With this preliminary definition the act proceeds to describe a number of offenses, embracing the teaching of criminal syndicalism, the printing or distribution of books, pamphlets, etc., advocating that doctrine, the organization of a society or assemblage which advocates it, and presiding at or assisting in conducting a meeting of such an organization, society or group. The prohibited acts are made felonies, punishable by imprisonment for not less than one year nor more than ten years, or by a fine of not more than $1,000, or by both.

We are concerned with but one of the described offenses and with the validity of the statute in this particular application. The charge is that appellant assisted in the conduct of a meeting which was called under the auspices of the Communist Party, an organization advocating criminal syndicalism. The defense was that the meeting was public and orderly and was held for a lawful purpose; that, while it was held under the auspices of the Communist Party, neither criminal syndicalism nor any unlawful conduct was taught or advocated at the meeting either by appellant or by others. Appellant moved for a direction of acquittal, contending that the statute as applied to him, for merely assisting at a meeting called by the Communist Party at which nothing unlawful was done or advocated, violated the due process clause of the Fourteenth Amendment of the Constitution of the United States.

This contention was overruled. Appellant was found guilty as charged and was sentenced to imprisonment for seven years. The judgment was affirmed by the Supreme Court of the State which considered the constitutional question and sustained the statute as thus applied. The case comes here on appeal. . . .

Stipulation of Facts

The stipulation, after setting forth the charging part of the indictment, recites in substance the following: That on July 27, 1934, there was held in Portland a meeting which had been advertised by handbills issued by the Portland section of the Communist Party; that the number of persons in attendance was variously estimated at from 150 to 300; that some of those present, who were members of the Communist Party, estimated that not to exceed 10 to 15 percent of those in attendance were such members; that the meeting was open to the public without charge and no questions were asked of those entering, with respect to their relation to the Communist Party; that the notice of the meeting advertised it as a protest against illegal raids on workers' halls and homes and against the shooting of striking longshoremen by Portland police; that the chairman stated that it was a meeting held by the Communist Party; that the first speaker dwelt on the activities of the Young Communist League; that the defendant De Jonge, the second speaker, was a member of the Communist Party and went to the meeting to speak in its name; that in his talk he protested against conditions in the county jail, the action of city police in relation to the maritime strike then in progress in Portland, and numerous other matters; that he discussed the reason for the raids on the Communist headquarters and workers' halls and offices; that he told the workers that these attacks were due to efforts on the part of the steamship companies and stevedoring companies to break the maritime longshoremen's and seamen's strike; that they hoped to break the strike by pitting the longshoremen and seamen against the Communist movement; that there was also testimony to the effect that defendant asked those present to do more work in obtaining members for the Communist Party and requested all to be at the meeting of the party to be held in Portland on the following evening and to bring their friends to show their defiance to local police authority and to assist them in their revolutionary tactics; that there was also testimony that defendant urged the purchase of certain communist literature which was sold at the meeting; that while the meeting was still in progress it was raided by the police; that the meeting was conducted in an orderly manner; that defendant and several others who were actively conducting the meeting were arrested by the police; and that on searching the hall the police found a quantity of communist literature.

The stipulation then set forth various extracts from the literature of the Communist Party to show its advocacy of criminal syndicalism. The stipulation does not disclose any activity by the defendant as a basis for his prosecution other than his participation in the meeting in question. Nor does the stipulation show that the communist literature distributed at the meeting contained any advocacy of criminal syndicalism or of any unlawful conduct. It was admitted by the Attorney General of the State in his argument at the bar of this Court that the literature distributed in the meeting was not of that sort and that the extracts contained in the stipulation were taken from communist literature found elsewhere. Its introduction in evidence was for the purpose of showing that the Communist Party as such did advocate the doctrine of criminal syndicalism, a fact which is not disputed on this appeal.

The Indictment

While the stipulation of facts is but a condensed statement, still much of it is irrelevant in the light of the particular charge of the indictment as construed by the Supreme Court. The indictment charged as follows:

> The said Dirk De Jonge, Don Cluster, Edward R. Denny and Earl Stewart on the 27th day of July, A.D., 1934, in the county of Multnomah and state of Oregon, then and there being, did then and there unlawfully and feloniously preside at, conduct and assist in conducting an assemblage of persons, organization, society and group, to wit: The Communist Party, a more particular description of which said assemblage of persons, organization, society and group is to this grand jury unknown, which said assemblage of persons, organization, society and group did then and there unlawfully and feloniously teach and advocate the doctrine of criminal syndicalism and sabotage, contrary to the statutes in such cases made and provided, and against the peace and dignity of the state of Oregon.

The State Courts' Interpretation

On the theory that this was a charge that criminal syndicalism and sabotage were advocated at the meeting in question, the defendant moved for acquittal, insisting that the evidence was insufficient to warrant his conviction. The trial court denied his motion, and error in this respect was assigned on appeal. The Supreme Court of the State put aside that contention by ruling that the indictment did not charge that criminal syndicalism or sabotage was advocated at the meeting described in the evidence, either by defendant or by anyone else. The words of the indictment that "said assemblage of persons, organiza-

tion, society, and group did then and there unlawfully and fe-
loniously teach and advocate the doctrine of criminal syndicalism and sabotage," referred not to the meeting in question,
or to anything then and there said or done by defendant or
others, but to the advocacy of criminal syndicalism and sabotage by the Communist Party in Multnomah County. The ruling of the state court upon this point was precise. The court
said:

> Turning now to the grounds for a directed verdict set forth
> in defendant's motion therefor, we note that he asserts and
> argues that the indictment charges the assemblage at which
> he spoke with unlawfully and feloniously teaching and ad-
> vocating the doctrine of criminal syndicalism and sabotage,
> and elsewhere in the same motion he contends that the in-
> dictment charges the defendant with unlawfully and feloni-
> ously teaching and advocating said doctrine at said meeting.
> The indictment does not, however, charge the defendant,
> nor the assemblage, at which he spoke, with teaching or ad-
> vocating at said meeting at 68 Southwest Alder Street, in the
> city of Portland, the doctrine of criminal syndicalism or
> sabotage. What the indictment does charge, in plain and
> concise language, is that the defendant presided at, con-
> ducted and assisted in conducting an assemblage of persons,
> organization, society, and group, to wit, the Communist
> Party which said assemblage of persons, organization, soci-
> ety, and group was unlawfully teaching and advocating in
> Multnomah county the doctrine of criminal syndicalism
> and sabotage.

In this view, lack of sufficient evidence as to illegal advocacy or action at the meeting became immaterial. Having limited the charge to defendant's participation in a meeting called
by the Communist Party, the state court sustained the conviction upon that basis regardless of what was said or done at
the meeting.

An Excessively Broad Statute

We must take the indictment as thus construed. Conviction upon a charge not made would be sheer denial of due process. It thus appears that, while defendant was a member of the Communist Party, he was not indicted for participating in its organization, or for joining it, or for soliciting members or for distributing its literature. He was not charged with teaching or advocating criminal syndicalism or sabotage or any unlawful acts, either at the meeting or elsewhere. He was accordingly deprived of the benefit of evidence as to the orderly and lawful conduct of the meeting and that it was not called or used for the advocacy of criminal syndicalism or sabotage or any unlawful action. His sole offense as charged, and for which he was convicted and sentenced to imprisonment for seven years, was that he had assisted in the conduct of a public meeting, albeit otherwise lawful, which was held under the auspices of the Communist Party.

The broad reach of the statute as thus applied is plain. While defendant was a member of the Communist Party, that membership was not necessary to conviction on such a charge. A like fate might have attended any speaker, although not a member who "assisted in the conduct" of the meeting. However innocuous the object of the meeting, however lawful the subjects and tenor of the addresses, however reasonable and timely the discussion, all those assisting in the conduct of the meeting would be subject to imprisonment as felons if the meeting were held by the Communist Party. This manifest result was brought out sharply at this bar by the concessions which the Attoney General made, and could not avoid, in the light of the decision of the state court. Thus, if the Communist Party had called a public meeting in Portland to discuss the tariff, or the foreign policy of the government, or taxation, or relief, or candidacies for the offices of President, members of Congress, Governor, or state legislators, every speaker who assisted in the conduct of the meeting would be equally guilty with the defendant in this case, upon the charge as here defined and sustained. The list of illustrations might be indefinitely extended to every variety of meetings under the auspices of the Communist Party although held for the discussion of political issues or to adopt protests and pass resolutions of an entirely innocent and proper character.

While the States are entitled to protect themselves from the abuse of the privileges of our institutions through an attempted substitution of force and violence in the place of peaceful political action in order to effect revolutionary changes in government, none of our decisions go to the length of sustaining such a curtailment of the right of free speech and assembly as the Oregon statute demands in its present application. In *Gitlow v. People of State of New York*, under the New York statute defining criminal anarchy, the defendant was found to be responsible for a "manifesto" advocating the overthrow of the government by violence and unlawful means. In *Whitney v. People of State of California*, under the California statute relating to criminal syndicalism, the defendant was found guilty of willfully and deliberately assisting in the forming of an organization for the purpose of carrying on a revolutionary class struggle by criminal methods. The defendant was convicted of participation in what amounted to a conspiracy to commit serious crimes. The case of *Burns v. United States*, involved a similar ruling under the California statute as extended to the Yosemite National Park. On the other hand, in *Fiske v. Kansas*, the criminal syndicalism act of that State was held to have been applied unconstitutionally and the judgment of conviction was reversed, where it was not shown that unlawful methods had been advocated.

Right of Assembly Is Fundamental

Freedom of speech and of the press are fundamental rights which are safeguarded by the due process clause of the Fourteenth Amendment of the Federal Constitution. The right of peaceable assembly is a right cognate to those of free speech and free press and is equally fundamental. As this Court said in *United States v. Cruikshank*, "The very idea of a government, republican in form, implies a right on the part of its citizens to meet peaceably for consultation in respect to public affairs and to petition for a redress of grievances." The First Amendment of the Federal Constitution expressly guarantees that right against abridgment by Congress. But explicit mention there does not argue exclusion elsewhere. For the right is one that cannot be denied without violating those fundamental principles of liberty and justice which lie at the base of all civil and political institutions—principles which the Fourteenth Amendment embodies in the general terms of its due process clause.

These rights may be abused by using speech or press or assembly in order to incite to violence and crime. The people through their Legislatures may protect themselves against that abuse. But the legislative intervention can find constitutional justification only by dealing with the abuse. The rights themselves must not be curtailed. The greater the importance of safeguarding the community from incitements to the overthrow of our institutions by force and violence, the more imperative is the need to preserve inviolate the constitutional rights of free speech, free press and free assembly in order to maintain the opportunity for free political discussion, to the end that government may be responsive to the will of the people and that changes, if desired, may be obtained by peaceful means. Therein lies the security of the Republic, the very foundation of constitutional government.

Peaceable Assembly Cannot Be a Crime

It follows from these considerations that, consistent with the Federal Constitution, peaceable assembly for lawful discussion cannot be made a crime. The holding of meetings for peaceable political action cannot be proscribed. Those who assist in the conduct of such meetings cannot be branded as criminals on that score. The question, if the rights of free speech and peaceable assembly are to be preserved, is not as to the auspices under which the meeting is held but as to its purpose; not as to the relations of the speakers, but whether their utterances transcend the bounds of the freedom of speech which the Constitution protects. If the persons assembling have committed crimes elsewhere, if they have formed or are engaged in a conspiracy against the public peace and order, they may be prosecuted for their conspiracy or other violation of valid laws. But it is a different matter when the State, instead of prosecuting them for such offenses, seizes upon mere participation in a peaceable assembly and a lawful public discussion as the basis for a criminal charge.

We are not called upon to review the findings of the state court as to the objectives of the Communist Party. Notwithstanding those objectives, the defendant still enjoyed his personal right of free speech and to take part in a peaceable assembly having a lawful purpose, although called by that party. The defendant was none the less entitled to discuss the public issues of the day and thus in a lawful manner, without incitement to violence or crime, to seek redress of alleged grievances. That was of the essence of his guaranteed personal liberty.

We hold that the Oregon statute as applied to the particular charge as defined by the state court is repugnant to the due process clause of the Fourteenth Amendment. The judgment of conviction is reversed and the cause is remanded for further proceedings not inconsistent with this opinion.

Unions Have the Right to Picket

Frank Murphy

One of the more important forms of assembly is picketing, in which groups of people gather to protest the actions of a corporation or organization by marching in front of a building. However, early in the twentieth century, picketing was illegal in many states under legislation designed to hinder unionization. In 1923, Alabama passed a statute against picketing, broadly defined to prevent anyone without a "just cause" from loitering near a lawful business with the purpose of hindering its operations or influencing the public either to boycott its products or decline to work there.

In 1940 the case of Byron Thornhill, a union president arrested and jailed for participating in a picket line, came before the U.S. Supreme Court. In an 8-to-1 decision, the Court found in Thornhill v. Alabama *that the statute fundamentally violated Thornhill's right to peaceably assemble with like-minded workers as well as his right to petition for redress of grievances. As Justice Frank Murphy explains in the majority opinion, excerpted below, the vague and sweeping language of the statute could not be justified as an attempt to prevent breaches of the peace. Instead, it closed off nearly every avenue that workers or unions had to educate the public about their grievances in a peaceful and effective way.*

A onetime child worker in a factory, Murphy developed a strong sympathy for the underprivileged. As mayor of Detroit and governor of Michigan during the Great Depression he earned national recognition for his attempts to alleviate unemployment. In 1939 he became President Franklin D. Roosevelt's attorney general, and a year later the president appointed him to the Supreme Court, where he served until his death in 1949.

Frank Murphy, majority opinion, *Thornhill v. State of Alabama*, 310 U.S. 88, April 22, 1940.

Petitioner, Byron Thornhill, was convicted in the Circuit Court of Tuscaloosa County, Alabama, of the violation of Section 3448 of the State Code of 1923. The Code Section reads as follows: "3448. Loitering or picketing forbidden. Any person or persons, who, without a just cause or legal excuse therefor, go near to or loiter about the premises or place of business of any other person, firm, corporation, or association of people, engaged in a lawful business, for the purpose, or with intent of influencing, or inducing other persons not to trade with, buy from, sell to, have business dealings with, or be employed by such persons, firm, corporation, or association, or who picket the works or place of business of such other persons, firms, corporations, or associations of persons, for the purpose of hindering, delaying, or interfering with or injuring any lawful business or enterprise of another, shall be guilty of a misdemeanor; but nothing herein shall prevent any person from soliciting trade or business for a competitive business."

The complaint against petitioner ... is phrased substantially in the very words of the statute. The first and second counts charge that petitioner, without just cause or legal excuse, did "go near to or loiter about the premises" of the Brown Wood Preserving Company with the intent or purpose of influencing others to adopt one of [the] enumerated courses of conduct. In the third count, the charge is that petitioner "did picket" the works of the Company "for the purpose of hindering, delaying or interfering with or injuring (its) lawful business." Petitioner demurred to the complaint on the grounds, among others, that Section 3448 was repugnant to the Constitution of the United States (Amendment 1) in that it deprived him of "the right of peaceful assemblage," "the right of freedom of speech," and "the right to petition for redress." The demurrer, so far as the record shows, was not ruled upon, and petitioner pleaded not guilty. The Circuit Court then proceeded to try the case without a jury, one not

51

being asked for or demanded. At the close of the case for the State, petitioner moved to exclude all the testimony taken at the trial on the ground that Section 3448 was violative of the Constitution of the United States. The Circuit Court overruled the motion, found petitioner "guilty of Loitering and Picketing as charged in the complaint," and entered judgment accordingly. The judgment was affirmed by the Court of Appeals, which considered the constitutional question and sustained the section on the authority of two previous decisions in the Alabama courts. . . .

Key Issues Before the Court

The freedom of speech and of the press, which are secured by the First Amendment against abridgment by the United States, are among the fundamental personal rights and liberties which are secured to all persons by the Fourteenth Amendment against abridgment by a state. . . .

A . . . threat is inherent in a penal statute, like that in question here, which does not aim specifically at evils within the allowable area of State control but, on the contrary, sweeps within its ambit other activities that in ordinary circumstances constitute an exercise of freedom of speech or of the press. The existence of such a statute, which readily lends itself to harsh and discriminatory enforcement by local prosecuting officials, against particular groups deemed to merit their displeasure, results in a continuous and pervasive restraint on all freedom of discussion that might reasonably be regarded as within its purview. It is not any less effective or, if the restraint is not permissible, less pernicious than the restraint on freedom of discussion imposed by the threat of censorship. . . .

No Room for Reasonable Exceptions

Section 3448 has been applied by the State courts so as to prohibit a single individual from walking slowly and peacefully back and forth on the public sidewalk in front of the premises of an employer, without speaking to anyone, carrying a sign or placard on a staff above his head stating only the fact that the employer did not employ union men affiliated with the American Federation of Labor; the purpose of the described activity was concededly to advise customers and prospective customers of the relationship existing between the employer and its employees and thereby to induce such customers not to patronize the employer. The statute as thus authoritatively construed and applied leaves room for no exceptions based upon either the number of persons engaged in the proscribed activity, the peaceful character of their demeanor, the nature of their dispute with an employer, or the restrained character and the accurateness of the terminology used in notifying the public of the facts of the dispute.

The numerous forms of conduct proscribed by Section 3448 are subsumed under two offenses: the first embraces the activities of all who "without a just cause or legal excuse" "go near to or loiter about the premises" of any person engaged in a lawful business for the purpose of influencing or inducing others to adopt any of certain enumerated courses of action; the second, all who "picket" the place of business of any such person "for the purpose of hindering, delaying, or interfering with or injuring any lawful business or enterprise of another." It is apparent that one or the other of the offenses comprehends every practicable method whereby the facts of a labor dispute may be publicized in the vicinity of the place of business of an employer. The phrase "without a just cause or legal excuse" does not in any effective manner restrict the breadth of the regulation; the words themselves have no ascertainable meaning either inherent or historical. The courses of action, listed under the first offense, which an accused—including an employee—may not urge others to take, comprehends those which in many instances would normally result from merely publicizing, without annoyance or threat of any kind, the facts of a labor dispute. An intention to hinder, delay or interfere with a lawful business, which is an element of the second offense, likewise can be proved merely by showing that others reacted in a way normally expectable of some upon learning the facts of a dispute. The vague contours of the term "picket" are nowhere delineated. Employees or others, accordingly, may be found to be within the purview of the term and convicted for engaging in activities identical with those proscribed by the first offense. In sum, whatever the means used to publicize the facts of a labor dispute, whether by printed sign, by pamphlet, by word of mouth or otherwise, all such activity without exception is within the inclusive prohibition of the statute so long as it occurs in the vicinity of the scene of the dispute. . . .

Invalid on Its Face

We think that Section 3448 is invalid on its face.

The freedom of speech and of the press guaranteed by the Constitution embraces at the least the liberty to discuss publicly and truthfully all matters of public concern without previous restraint or fear of subsequent punishment. The exigencies of the colonial period and the efforts to secure freedom from oppressive administration developed a broadened conception of these liberties as adequate to supply the public need for information and education with respect to the significant issues of the times. The Continental Congress in its letter sent to the Inhabitants of Quebec (October 26, 1774) referred to the "five great rights" and said: "The last right we shall mention, regards the freedom of the press. The importance of this consists, besides the advancement of truth, science, morality, and arts in general, in its diffusion of liberal sentiments on the administration of Government, its ready communication of thoughts between subjects, and its consequential promotion of union among them, whereby oppressive officers are shamed or intimidated, into more honourable and just modes of conducting affairs." Freedom of discussion,

United Auto Workers president Douglas Fraser (foreground) walks the picket line in support of striking air traffic controllers at Detroit Metropolitan Airport in 1981. ©
Bettmann/Corbis

if it would fulfill its historic function in this nation, must embrace all issues about which information is needed or appropriate to enable the members of society to cope with the exigencies of their period.

In the circumstances of our times the dissemination of information concerning the facts of a labor dispute must be regarded as within that area of free discussion that is guaranteed by the Constitution. It is recognized now that satisfactory hours and wages and working conditions in industry and a bargaining position which makes these possible have an importance which is not less than the interests of those in the business or industry directly concerned. The health of the present generation and of those as yet unborn may depend on these matters, and the practices in a single factory may have economic repercussions upon a whole region and affect widespread systems of marketing. The merest glance at State and Federal legislation on the subject demonstrates the force of the argument that labor relations are not matters of mere local or private concern. Free discussion concerning the conditions in industry and the causes of labor disputes appears to us indispensable to the effective and intelligent use of the processes of popular government to shape the destiny of modern industrial society. The issues raised by regulations, such as are challenged here, infringing upon the right of employees effectively to inform the public of the facts of a labor dispute are part of this larger problem. We concur in the observation of Mr. Justice Brandeis, speaking for the Court in [*Senn v. Tile Layers Union* (1937)]: "Members of a union might, without special statutory authorization by a state, make known the facts of a labor dispute, for freedom of speech is guaranteed by the Federal Constitution."

The State Cannot Impair
Truthful Discussion

It is true that the rights of employers and employees to conduct their economic affairs and to compete with others for a share in the products of industry are subject to modification or qualification in the interests of the society in which they exist. This is but an instance of the power of the State to set the limits of permissible contest open to industrial combatants. It does not follow that the State in dealing with the evils arising from industrial disputes may impair the effective exercise of the right to discuss freely industrial relations which are matters of public concern. A contrary conclusion could be used to support abridgment of freedom of speech and of the press concerning almost every matter of importance to society.

The range of activities proscribed by Section 3448, whether characterized as picketing or loitering or otherwise, embraces nearly every practicable, effective means whereby those interested—including the employees directly affected—may enlighten the public on the nature and causes of a labor dispute. The safeguarding of these means is essential to the securing of an informed and educated public opinion with respect to a matter which is of public concern. It may be that effective exercise of the means of advancing public knowledge may persuade some of those reached to refrain from entering into advantageous relations with the business establishment which is the scene of the dispute. Every expression of opinion on matters that are important has the potentiality of inducing action in the interests of one rather than another group in society. But the group in power at any moment may not impose penal sanctions on peaceful and truthful discussion of matters of public interest merely on a showing that others may thereby be persuaded to take action inconsistent with its interests. Abridgment of the liberty of such discussion can be justified only where the clear danger of substantive evils arises under circumstances affording no opportunity to test the merits of ideas by competition for acceptance in the market of public opinion. We hold that the danger of injury to an industrial concern is neither so serious nor so imminent as to justify the sweeping proscription of freedom of discussion embodied in Section 3448.

No Clear and Present Danger

The State urges that the purpose of the challenged statute is the protection of the community from the violence and breaches of the peace, which, it asserts, are the concomitants of picketing. The power and the duty of the State to take adequate steps to preserve the peace and to protect the privacy, the lives, and the property of its residents cannot be doubted. But no clear and present danger of destruction of life or property, or invasion of the right of privacy, or breach of the peace can be thought to be inherent in the activities of every person who approaches the premises of an employer and publicizes the facts of a labor dispute involving the latter. We are not now concerned with picketing en masse or otherwise conducted which might occasion such imminent and aggravated danger to these interests as to justify a statute narrowly drawn to cover the precise situation giving rise to the danger. Section 3448 in question here does not aim specifically at serious encroachments on these interests and does not evidence any such care in balancing these interests against the interest of the community and that of the individual in freedom of discussion on matters of public concern.

It is not enough to say that Section 3448 is limited or restricted in its application to such activity as takes place at the scene of the labor dispute. "[The] streets are natural and proper places for the dissemination of information and opinion; and one is not to have the exercise of his liberty of expression in appropriate places abridged on the plea that it may be exercised in some other place." The danger of breach of the peace or serious invasion of rights of property or privacy at the scene of a labor dispute is not sufficiently imminent in all cases to warrant the legislature in determining that such place is not appropriate for the range of activities outlawed by Section 3448.

Government Can Limit the Freedom of Assembly

Charles Evans Hughes

The Jehovah's Witnesses is a religion, founded in the 1870s, whose tenets include a strong belief in the imminent end of the world. In addition, its stance on a number of issues, such as a refusal to say the Pledge of Allegiance or to undergo blood transfusions, sets it apart from many other Christian churches. In the 1930s, under the leadership of Joseph Franklin Rutherford, the sect experienced rapid growth through energetic evangelization, often combined with vigorous denunciations of other Christian denominations and modern governments. This aspect of the church's faith sometimes led to confrontations with other citizens or with local officials.

In 1939 a group of Jehovah's Witnesses decided to hold a demonstration in Manchester, New Hampshire. Five groups of fifteen to twenty members marched in formation carrying signs with statements such as "Religion Is a Snare and a Racket." Local officials arrested most of the participants under a statute that forbade parading without a license. The defendants appealed their case to the U.S. Supreme Court based on a belief that their First Amendment right to peaceable assembly had been violated.

In Cox v. New Hampshire, *a unanimous Court found that the right to assemble had reasonable limitations and that the local officials had acted within those limitations. In the following excerpt from his opinion in the case, Charles Evans Hughes contends that the law requiring a parade license did not violate the defendants' rights and was justified on the grounds of public order and safety. Although the Court found against the defendants on the narrow grounds at issue, it affirmed that restrictions on assembly could not be unreasonable or designed to suppress a particular organization's or individual's right to free expression.*

Charles Evans Hughes, majority opinion, *Cox v. New Hampshire*, 312 U.S. 569, March 31, 1941.

Hughes served two terms on the Supreme Court. He was first appointed as a justice by President William Taft in 1910, but he resigned in 1916 to run as the Republican Party nominee for president. In 1930 President Herbert Hoover reappointed him to the Court, this time as chief justice, a position he held until his resignation in 1941.

Appellants are five "Jehovah's Witnesses" who, with sixty-three others of the same persuasion, were convicted in the municipal court of Manchester, New Hampshire, for violation of a state statute prohibiting a "parade or procession" upon a public street without a special license.

Upon appeal, there was a trial de novo [a new trial] of these appellants before a jury in the Superior Court, the other defendants having agreed to abide by the final decision in that proceeding. Appellants were found guilty and the judgment of conviction was affirmed by the Supreme Court of the State.

By motions and exceptions, appellants raised the questions that the statute was invalid under the Fourteenth Amendment of the Constitution of the United States in that it deprived appellants of their rights of freedom of worship, freedom of speech and press, and freedom of assembly, vested unreasonable and unlimited arbitrary and discriminatory powers in the licensing authority, and was vague and indefinite. These contentions were overruled and the case comes here on appeal.

The statutory prohibition is as follows: "No theatrical or dramatic representation shall be performed or exhibited, and no parade or procession upon any public street or way, and no open-air public meeting upon any ground abutting thereon, shall be permitted, unless a special license therefor shall first be obtained from the selectmen of the town, or from a licensing committee for cities hereinafter provided for." . . .

Facts of the Case

The facts, which are conceded by the appellants to be established by the evidence, are these: The sixty-eight defendants and twenty other persons met at a hall in the City of Manchester on the evening of Saturday, July 8, 1939, "for the purpose of engaging in an information march." The company was divided into four or five groups, each with about fifteen to twenty persons. Each group then proceeded to a different part of the business district of the city and there "would line up in single-file formation and then proceed to march along the sidewalk, 'single-file', that is, following one another." Each of the defendants carried a small staff with a sign reading "Religion is a Snare and a Racket" and on the reverse "Serve God and Christ the King." Some of the marchers carried placards bearing the statement "Fascism or Freedom. Hear Judge Rutherford and Face the Facts." The marchers also handed out printed leaflets announcing a meeting to be held at a later time in the hall from which they had started, where a talk on government would be given to the public free of charge. Defendants did not apply for a permit and none was issued.

There was a dispute in the evidence as to the distance between the marchers. Defendants said that they were from fifteen to twenty feet apart. The State insists that the evidence clearly showed that the "marchers were as close together as it was possible for them to walk." Appellants concede that this dispute is not material to the questions presented. The recital of facts which prefaced the opinion of the state court thus summarizes the effect of the march: "Manchester had a population of over 75,000 in 1930, and there was testimony that on Saturday nights in an hour's time 26,000 persons passed one of the intersections where the defendants marched. The marchers interfered with the normal sidewalk travel, but no technical breach of the peace occurred. The march was a prearranged affair, and no permit for it was sought, although the defendants understood that under the statute one was required."

Appellants urge that each of the defendants was a minister ordained to preach the gospel in accordance with his belief and that the participation of these ministers in the march was for the purpose of disseminating information in the public interest and was one of their ways of worship.

The Sole Charge

The sole charge against appellants was that they were "taking part in a parade or procession" on public streets without a permit as the statute required. They were not prosecuted for distributing leaflets, or for conveying information by placards or otherwise, or for issuing invitations to a public meeting, or for holding a public meeting, or for maintaining or expressing religious beliefs. Their right to do any one of these things apart from engaging in a "parade or procession" upon a public street is not here involved and the question of the validity of a statute addressed to any other sort of conduct than that complained of is not before us.

There appears to be no ground for challenging the ruling of the state court that appellants were in fact engaged in a parade or procession upon the public streets. As the state court observed: "It was a march in formation, and its advertising and informatory purpose did not make it otherwise.... It is immaterial that its tactics were few and simple. It is enough that it proceeded in ordered and close file as a collective body of persons on the city streets."

Civil Liberties Imply Organized Society

Civil liberties, as guaranteed by the Constitution, imply the existence of an organized society maintaining public order without which liberty itself would be lost in the excesses of unrestrained abuses. The authority of a municipality to impose regulations in order to assure the safety and convenience of the people in the use of public highways has never been regarded as inconsistent with civil liberties but rather as one of the means of safeguarding the good order upon which they ultimately depend. The control of travel on the streets of cities is the most familiar illustration of this recognition of social need. Where a restriction of the use of highways in that relation is designed to promote the public convenience in the interest of all, it cannot be disregarded by the attempted exercise of some civil right which in other circumstances would be entitled to protection. One would not be justified in ignoring the familiar red traffic light because he thought it his religious duty to disobey the municipal command or sought by that means to direct public attention to an announcement of his opinions. As regulation of the use of the streets for parades and processions is a traditional exercise of control by local government, the question in a particular case is whether that control is exerted so as not to deny or unwarrantedly abridge the right of assembly and the opportunities for the communication of thought and the discussion of public questions immemorially associated with resort to public places.

Slight Interference with Liberty

In the instant case [i.e., the case under consideration], we are aided by the opinion of the Supreme Court of the State which construed the statute and defined the limitations of the authority conferred for the granting of licenses for parades and processions. The court observed that if the clause of the Act requiring a license "for all open-air public meetings upon land contiguous to a highway" was invalid, that invalidity did not nullify the Act in its application to the other situations described. Recognizing the importance of the civil liberties invoked by appellants, the court thought it significant that the statute prescribed "no measures for controlling or suppressing the publication on the highways of facts and opinions, either by speech or by writing"; that communication "by the distribution of literature or by the display of placards and signs" was in no respect regulated by the statute; that the regulation with respect to parades and processions was applicable only "to organized formations of persons using the highways"; and that "the defendants separately or collectively in groups not constituting a parade or procession," were "under no contemplation of the act." In this light, the court thought that interference with liberty of speech and writing seemed slight; that the distribution of pamphlets and folders by the groups "traveling in unorganized fashion" would have had as large a circulation, and that "signs carried by members of the groups not in marching formation would have been as conspicuous, as published by them while in parade or procession."

It was with this view of the limited objective of the statute that the state court considered and defined the duty of the licensing authority and the rights of the appellants to a license for their parade, with regard only to considerations of time, place and manner so as to conserve the public convenience. The obvious advantage of requiring application for a permit was noted as giving the public authorities notice in advance so as to afford opportunity for proper policing. And the court further observed that, in fixing time and place, the license served "to prevent confusion by overlapping parades or processions, to secure convenient use of the streets by other travelers, and to minimize the risk of disorder." But the court held that the licensing board was not vested with arbitrary power or an unfettered discretion; that its discretion must be exercised with "uniformity of method of treatment upon the facts of each application, free from improper or inappropriate considerations and from unfair discrimination"; that a "systematic, consistent and just order of treatment, with reference to the convenience of public use of the highways, is the statutory mandate." The defendants, said the court, "had a right, under the act, to a license to march when, where and as they did, if after a required investigation it was found that the convenience of the public in the use of the streets would not thereby be unduly disturbed, upon such conditions or changes in time, place and manner as would avoid disturbance."

No Violation of Constitutional Rights

If a municipality has authority to control the use of its public streets for parades or processions, as it undoubtedly has, it cannot be denied authority to give consideration, without unfair discrimination, to time, place and manner in relation to the other proper uses of the streets. We find it impossible to say that the limited authority conferred by the licensing provisions of the statute in question as thus construed by the state court contravened any constitutional right.

There remains the question of license fees which, as the court said, had a permissible range from $300 to a nominal amount. The court construed the Act as requiring "a reasonable fixing of the amount of the fee." "The charge," said the court, "for a circus parade or a celebration procession of length, each drawing crowds of observers, would take into account the greater public expense of policing the spectacle, compared with the slight expense of a less expansive and attractive parade or procession, to which the charge would be adjusted." The fee was held to be "not a revenue tax, but one to meet the expense incident to the administration of the act and to the maintenance of public order in the matter licensed." There is nothing contrary to the Constitution in the charge of a fee limited to the purpose stated. The suggestion that a flat fee should have been charged fails to take account of the difficulty of framing a fair schedule to meet all circumstances, and we perceive no constitutional ground for denying to local governments that flexibility of adjustment of fees which in the light of varying conditions would tend to conserve rather than impair the liberty sought.

There is no evidence that the statute has been administered otherwise than in the fair and non-discriminatory manner which the state court has construed it to require.

Previous Cases Do Not Apply

The decisions upon which appellants rely are not applicable. In *Lovell v. Griffin*, the ordinance prohibited the distribution of literature of any kind at any time, at any place, and in any manner without a permit from the city manager, thus striking at the very foundation of the freedom of the press by subjecting it to license and censorship. In *Hague v. Committee for Industrial Organization*, the ordinance dealt with the exercise of the right of assembly for the purpose of communicating views; it did not make comfort or convenience in the use of streets the standard of official action but enabled the local official absolutely to refuse a permit on his mere opinion that such refusal would prevent "riots, disturbances or disorderly assemblage." The ordinance thus created, as the record disclosed, an instrument of arbitrary suppression of opinions on public questions. The court said that "uncontrolled official suppression of the privilege cannot be made a substitute for the duty to maintain order in connection with the exercise of the right." In *Schneider v. State*, the ordinance was directed at canvassing and banned unlicensed communication of any views, or the advocacy of any cause, from door to door, subject only to the power of a police officer to determine as a censor what literature might be distributed and who might distribute it. In *Cantwell v. Connecticut*, the statute dealt with the solicitation of funds for religious causes and authorized an official to determine whether the cause was a religious one and to refuse a permit if he determined it was not, thus establishing a censorship of religion.

Nor is any question of peaceful picketing here involved, as in *Thornhill v. Alabama* and *Carlson v. People of California*. The statute, as the state court said, is not aimed at any restraint of freedom of speech, and there is no basis for an assumption that it would be applied so as to prevent peaceful picketing as described in the cases cited.

The argument as to freedom of worship is also beside the point. No interference with religious worship or the practice of religion in any proper sense is shown, but only the exercise of local control over the use of streets for parades and processions.

The judgment of the Supreme Court of New Hampshire is affirmed.

States May Not Interfere with the Freedom of Association

John M. Harlan

In the 1950s the long struggle to bring equal rights to African Americans took on a new urgency—in the courts as well as in the larger society. Organizations such as the National Association for the Advancement of Colored People (NAACP) were pressing, often successfully, for an end to segregation in the southern states. When the NAACP opened an office in Alabama, the state first tried to expel it. As part of the subsequent lawsuit, the state demanded that the NAACP turn over a number of documents, including its membership list. Fearing retribution for its members from white racists, including those in the state government, the NAACP withheld its list and was held in contempt. It appealed, and eventually the case went to the U.S. Supreme Court.

In its decision for NAACP v. Alabama, *a unanimous Supreme Court held that forcing the NAACP to release its membership list was unjustified and unconstitutional. In the Court's opinion, written by Justice John M. Harlan and excerpted below, the Court found that Alabama had no compelling interest in demanding the membership list. Instead, the assault on the privacy rights of the NAACP's members threatened their fundamental right to freely associate with like-minded individuals. In short, the state's actions were a violation of the First and Fourteenth Amendments and could not be allowed.*

John Marshall Harlan II was the grandson of another John Marshall Harlan, also a Supreme Court Justice, who had written a stirring dissent to the notorious 1898 decision of Plessy v. Ferguson, *which upheld segregation. The younger Harlan enjoyed a distinguished career as a lawyer and judge and in 1955 was ap-*

John M. Harlan, majority opinion, *N.A.A.C.P. v. Alabama*, 357 U.S. 449, June 30, 1958.

pointed by President Dwight D. Eisenhower to the Supreme Court. He retired in 1971 and died in December of that year.

We review from the standpoint of its validity under the Federal Constitution a judgment of civil contempt entered against petitioner, the National Association for the Advancement of Colored People, in the courts of Alabama. The question presented is whether Alabama, consistently with the Due Process Clause of the Fourteenth Amendment, can compel petitioner to reveal to the State's Attorney General the names and addresses of all its Alabama members and agents, without regard to their positions or functions in the Association. The judgment of contempt was based upon petitioner's refusal to comply fully with a court order requiring in part the production of membership lists. Petitioner's claim is that the order, in the circumstances shown by this record, violated rights assured to petitioner and its members under the Constitution. . . .

On Behalf of Members

The Association both urges that it is constitutionally entitled to resist official inquiry into its membership lists, and that it may assert, on behalf of its members, a right personal to them to be protected from compelled disclosure by the State of their affiliation with the Association as revealed by the membership lists. We think that petitioner argues more appropriately the rights of its members, and that its nexus with them is sufficient to permit that it act as their representative before this Court. In so concluding, we reject respondent's argument that the Association lacks standing to assert here constitutional rights pertaining to the members, who are not of course parties to the litigation.

To limit the breadth of issues which must be dealt with in particular litigation, this Court has generally insisted that parties rely only on constitutional rights which are personal to themselves. This rule is related to the broader doctrine that constitutional adjudication should where possible be avoided. The principle is not disrespected where constitutional rights of persons who are not immediately before the Court could not be effectively vindicated except through an appropriate representative before the Court.

If petitioner's rank-and-file members are constitutionally entitled to withhold their connection with the Association despite the production order, it is manifest that this right is properly assertable by the Association. To require that it be claimed by the members themselves would result in nullification of the right at the very moment of its assertion. Petitioner is the appropriate party to assert these rights, because it and its members are in every practical sense identical. The Association, which provides in its constitution that "[a]ny person who is in accordance with [its] principles and policies . . ." may become a member, is but the medium through which its individual members seek to make more effective the expression of their own views. The reasonable likelihood that the Association itself through diminished financial support and membership may be adversely affected if production is compelled is a further factor pointing towards our holding that petitioner has standing to complain of the production order on behalf of its members.

Disclosure Violates Lawful Association Rights

We thus reach petitioner's claim that the production order in the state litigation trespasses upon fundamental freedoms protected by the Due Process Clause of the Fourteenth Amendment. Petitioner argues that in view of the facts and circumstances shown in the record, the effect of compelled disclosure of the membership lists will be to abridge the rights of its rank-and-file members to engage in lawful association in support of their common beliefs. It contends that governmental action which, although not directly suppressing association, nevertheless carries this consequence, can be justified only upon some overriding valid interest of the State.

Effective advocacy of both public and private points of view, particularly controversial ones, is undeniably enhanced by group association, as this Court has more than once recognized by remarking upon the close nexus between the freedoms of speech and assembly. It is beyond debate that freedom to engage in association for the advancement of beliefs and ideas is an inseparable aspect of the "liberty" assured by the Due Process Clause of the Fourteenth Amendment, which embraces freedom of speech. Of course, it is immaterial whether the beliefs sought to be advanced by association pertain to political, economic, religious or cultural matters, and state action which may have the effect of curtailing the freedom to associate is subject to the closest scrutiny.

The fact that Alabama, so far as is relevant to the validity of the contempt judgment presently under review, has taken no direct action to restrict the right of petitioner's members to associate freely, does not end inquiry into the effect of the production order. In the domain of these indispensable liberties, whether of speech, press, or association, the decisions of this Court recognize that abridgment of such rights, even though unintended, may inevitably follow from varied forms of governmental action. Thus in [*American Communications Assn. v.*] *Douds*, the Court stressed that the legislation there challenged, which on its face sought to regulate labor unions and to secure stability in interstate commerce, would have the practical effect "of discouraging" the exercise of constitutionally protected political rights, and it upheld the statute only after concluding that the reasons advanced for its enactment were constitutionally sufficient to justify its possible deterrent effect upon such freedoms. Similar recognition of possible unconstitutional intimidation of the free exercise of the right to advocate underlay this Court's narrow construction of the authority of a congressional committee investigating lobbying and of an Act regulating lobbying, although in neither case was there an effort to suppress speech. The governmental action challenged may appear to be totally unrelated to protected liberties. Statutes imposing taxes upon rather than prohibiting particular activity have been struck down when perceived to have the consequence of unduly curtailing the liberty of freedom of press assured under the Fourteenth Amendment.

Privacy and the Freedom to Associate

It is hardly a novel perception that compelled disclosure of affiliation with groups engaged in advocacy may constitute as effective a restraint on freedom of association as the forms of governmental action in the cases above were thought likely to produce upon the particular constitutional rights there involved. This Court has recognized the vital relationship between freedom to associate and privacy in one's associations. When referring to the varied forms of governmental action which might interfere with freedom of assembly, it said in *American Communications Assn. v. Douds*: "A requirement that adherents of particular religious faiths or political parties wear identifying arm-bands, for example, is obviously of this nature." Compelled disclosure of membership in an organization engaged in advocacy of particular beliefs is of the same order. Inviolability of privacy in group association may in many circumstances be indispensable to preservation of freedom of association, particularly where a group espouses dissident beliefs.

We think that the production order, in the respects here drawn in question, must be regarded as entailing the likelihood of a substantial restraint upon the exercise by petitioner's members of their right to freedom of association. Petitioner has made an uncontroverted showing that on past occasions revelation of the identity of its rank-and-file members has exposed these members to economic reprisal, loss of employment, threat of physical coercion, and other manifestations of public hostility. Under these circumstances, we think it apparent that compelled disclosure of petitioner's Alabama membership is likely to affect adversely the ability of petitioner and its members to pursue their collective effort to foster beliefs which they admittedly have the right to advocate, in that it may induce members to withdraw from the Association and dissuade others from joining it because of fear of exposure of their beliefs shown through their associations and of the consequences of this exposure.

It is not sufficient to answer, as the State does here, that whatever repressive effect compulsory disclosure of names of petitioner's members may have upon participation by Alabama citizens in petitioner's activities follows not from state action but from private community pressures. The crucial factor is the interplay of governmental and private action, for it is only after the initial exertion of state power represented by the production order that private action takes hold.

Restrictions of Rights Unjustified

We turn to the final question whether Alabama has demonstrated an interest in obtaining the disclosures it seeks from petitioner which is sufficient to justify the deterrent effect which we have concluded these disclosures may well have on the free exercise by petitioner's members of their constitutionally protected right of association. . . . It is not of moment that the State has here acted solely through its judicial branch, for whether legislative or judicial, it is still the application of state power which we are asked to scrutinize.

It is important to bear in mind that petitioner asserts no right to absolute immunity from state investigation, and no right to disregard Alabama's laws. As shown by its substantial compliance with the production order, petitioner does not deny Alabama's right to obtain from it such information as the State desires concerning the purposes of the Association and its activities within the State. Petitioner has not objected to divulging the identity of its members who are employed by or hold official positions with it. It has urged the rights solely of its ordinary rank-and-file members. This is therefore not analogous to a case involving the interest of a State in protecting its citizens in their dealings with paid solicitors or agents of foreign corporations by requiring identification.

Whether there was "justification" in this instance turns solely on the substantiality of Alabama's interest in obtaining the membership lists. During the course of a hearing before the Alabama Circuit Court on a motion of petitioner to set aside the production order, the State Attorney General presented at length, under examination by petitioner, the State's reason for requesting the membership lists. The exclusive purpose was to determine whether petitioner was conducting intrastate business in violation of the Alabama foreign corporation registration statute, and the membership lists were expected to help resolve this question. The issues in the litigation commenced by Alabama by its bill in equity were whether the character of petitioner and its activities in Alabama had been such as to make petitioner subject to the registration statute, and whether the extent of petitioner's activities without qualifying suggested its permanent ouster from the State. Without intimating the slightest view upon the merits of these issues, we are unable to perceive that the disclosure of the names of petitioner's rank-and-file members has a substantial bearing on either of them. As matters stand in the state court, petitioner (1) has admitted its presence and conduct of activities in Alabama since 1918; (2) has offered to comply in all respects with the state qualification statute, although preserving its contention that the statute does not apply to it; and (3) has apparently complied satisfactorily with the production order, except for the membership lists, by furnishing the Attorney General with varied business records, its charter and statement of purposes, the names of all of its directors and officers, and with the total number of its Alabama members and the amount of their dues. These last items would not on this record appear subject to constitutional challenge and have been furnished, but whatever interest the State may have in obtaining names of ordinary members has not been shown to be sufficient to overcome petitioner's constitutional objections to the production order.

A Very Different Case

From what has already been said, we think it apparent that *Bryant v. Zimmerman* cannot be relied on in support of the State's position, for that case involved markedly different considerations in terms of the interest of the State in obtaining disclosure. There, this Court upheld, as applied to a member of a local chapter of the Ku Klux Klan, a New York statute requiring any unincorporated association which demanded an oath as a condition to membership to file with state officials copies of its ". . . constitution, by-laws, rules, regulations and oath of membership, together with a roster of its membership and a list of its officers for the current year." In its opinion, the Court took care to emphasize the nature of the organization which New York sought to regulate. The decision was based on the particular character of the Klan's activities, involving acts of unlawful intimidation and violence, which the Court assumed was before the state legislature when it enacted the statute, and of which the Court itself took judicial notice. Furthermore, the situation before us is significantly different from that in *Bryant*, because the organization there had made no effort to comply with any of the requirements of New York's statute but rather had refused to furnish the State with any information as to its local activities.

We hold that the immunity from state scrutiny of membership lists which the Association claims on behalf of its members is here so related to the right of the members to pursue their lawful private interests privately and to associate freely with others in so doing as to come within the protection of the Fourteenth Amendment. And we conclude that Alabama has fallen short of showing a controlling justification for the deterrent effect on the free enjoyment of the right to associate which disclosure of membership lists is likely to have. Accordingly, the judgment of civil contempt and the $100,000 fine which resulted from petitioner's refusal to comply with the production order in this respect must fall. . . .

For the reasons stated, the judgment of the Supreme Court of Alabama must be reversed and the case remanded for proceedings not inconsistent with this opinion.

The Boy Scouts Have the Right to Reject Gay Members

William H. Rehnquist

James Dale was an Eagle Scout and an assistant scoutmaster in the Boy Scouts of America (BSA), a youth organization designed to instill character and personal fitness in boys between seven and eighteen. While in college, Dale became a prominent spokesman for gay rights on campus. Shortly after a newspaper identified him as copresident of the Rutgers University Lesbian/Gay Alliance, he received a letter from the Boy Scouts revoking his position as assistant scoutmaster on the grounds that avowed homosexuals could not serve as adult leaders in the Scouts. He sued on the basis that the Boy Scouts had violated New Jersey's public accommodations statute by discriminating against gay members. After wending its way through the courts, the case reached the New Jersey Supreme Court, which found in favor of Dale, and was appealed to the U.S. Supreme Court by the BSA.

In Boy Scouts of America and Monmouth Council v. James Dale, *the Court ruled that the Boy Scouts had the right to reject James Dale as a member and a leader. The Court noted that the BSA had a mission to instill moral character in its members as a central part of its entire purpose. In addition, it had a clearly stated view that acceptance of homosexuality would violate its definition of morality. The Court found that requiring the BSA to accept an openly gay member, particularly in a leadership position, would effectively force the group to express a view that it clearly opposed, violating its right of "expressive association." The Court rejected the New Jersey Supreme Court's contention that BSA leaders could still express opposition to homosexuality even if they had an openly gay colleague. The Court thus upheld the right of individuals to associate with like-minded individu-*

William H. Rehnquist, majority opinion, *Boy Scouts of America and Monmouth Council v. James Dale*, 530 U.S. 640, June 28, 2000.

als—and not those in fundamental disagreement—and to form organizations that reflect and sustain their viewpoint.

After a distinguished, sometimes controversial career as a lawyer and assistant attorney general of the United States, William H. Rehnquist was nominated as an associate justice of the Supreme Court by President Richard Nixon in 1971. In 1986 he was elevated to the position of chief justice by President Ronald Reagan, a position he held until his death in 2005. In general, Rehnquist and the Court under his tenure were seen as conservative.

Petitioners are the Boy Scouts of America and the Monmouth Council, a division of the Boy Scouts of America (collectively, Boy Scouts). The Boy Scouts is a private, not-for-profit organization engaged in instilling its system of values in young people. The Boy Scouts asserts that homosexual conduct is inconsistent with the values it seeks to instill. Respondent is James Dale, a former Eagle Scout whose adult membership in the Boy Scouts was revoked when the Boy Scouts learned that he is an avowed homosexual and gay rights activist. The New Jersey Supreme Court held that New Jersey's public accommodations law requires that the Boy Scouts admit Dale. This case presents the question whether applying New Jersey's public accommodations law in this way violates the Boy Scouts' First Amendment right of expressive association. We hold that it does.

James Dale's Scouting History

James Dale entered scouting in 1978 at the age of eight by joining Monmouth Council's Cub Scout Pack 142. Dale became a Boy Scout in 1981 and remained a Scout until he turned 18. By all accounts, Dale was an exemplary Scout. In 1988, he achieved the rank of Eagle Scout, one of Scouting's highest honors.

Dale applied for adult membership in the Boy Scouts in 1989. The Boy Scouts approved his application for the position of assistant scoutmaster of Troop 73. Around the same time, Dale left home to attend Rutgers University. After arriving at Rutgers, Dale first acknowledged to himself and others that he is gay. He quickly became involved with, and eventually became the copresident of, the Rutgers University Lesbian/ Gay Alliance. In 1990, Dale attended a seminar addressing the psychological and health needs of lesbian and gay teenagers. A newspaper covering the event interviewed Dale about his advocacy of homosexual teenagers' need for gay role models. In early July 1990, the newspaper published the interview and Dale's photograph over a caption identifying him as the copresident of the Lesbian/Gay Alliance.

Later that month, Dale received a letter from Monmouth Council Executive James Kay revoking his adult membership. Dale wrote to Kay requesting the reason for Monmouth Council's decision. Kay responded by letter that the Boy Scouts "specifically forbid membership to homosexuals."

In 1992, Dale filed a complaint against the Boy Scouts in the New Jersey Superior Court. The complaint alleged that the Boy Scouts had violated New Jersey's public accommodations statute and its common law by revoking Dale's membership based solely on his sexual orientation. New Jersey's public accommodations statute prohibits, among other things, discrimination on the basis of sexual orientation in places of public accommodation. . . .

New Jersey Supreme Court Finds for Dale

The New Jersey Supreme Court . . . held that the Boy Scouts was a place of public accommodation subject to the public accommodations law, that the organization was not exempt from the law under any of its express exceptions, and that the Boy Scouts violated the law by revoking Dale's membership based on his avowed homosexuality. After considering the state-law issues, the court addressed the Boy Scouts' claims that application of the public accommodations law in this case violated its federal constitutional rights "'to enter into and maintain ... intimate or private relationships ... [and] to associate for the purpose of engaging in protected speech.'" With respect to the right to intimate association, the court concluded that the Boy Scouts' "large size, nonselectivity, inclusive rather than exclusive purpose, and practice of inviting or allowing nonmembers to attend meetings, establish that the organization is not 'sufficiently personal or private to warrant constitutional protection' under the freedom of intimate association." With respect to the right of expressive association, the court "agree[d] that Boy Scouts expresses a belief in moral values and uses its activities to encourage the moral development of its members." But the court concluded that it was "not persuaded ... that a shared goal of Boy Scout members is to associate in order to preserve the view that homosexuality is immoral." Accordingly, the court held "that Dale's membership does not violate the Boy Scouts' right of expressive association because his inclusion would not 'affect in any significant way [the Boy Scouts'] existing members' ability to carry out their various purposes.'" The court also determined that New Jersey has a compelling interest in eliminating "the destructive consequences of discrimination from our society," and that its public accommodations law abridges no more speech than is necessary to accomplish its purpose. Finally, the court addressed the Boy Scouts' reliance on *Hurley v. Irish-American Gay, Lesbian and Bisexual Group of Boston, Inc.* (1995) in support of its claimed First Amendment right to exclude Dale. The court determined that *Hurley* did not require deciding the case in favor of the Boy Scouts because "the reinstatement of Dale does not compel Boy Scouts to express any message."

We granted the Boy Scouts' petition for certiorari [i.e., to have the Supreme Court decide the case] to determine whether the application of New Jersey's public accommodations law violated the First Amendment.

Groups such as Scouting for All, protesting here at the Boy Scouts of America annual meeting in Chicago in 2004, say the Scouts discriminate against gays. © John Zich/ zrImages/Corbis

A Freedom Not to Associate

In *Roberts v. United States Jaycees* (1984), we observed that "implicit in the right to engage in activities protected by the First Amendment" is "a corresponding right to associate with others in pursuit of a wide variety of political, social, economic, educational, religious, and cultural ends." This right is crucial in preventing the majority from imposing its views on groups that would rather express other, perhaps unpopular, ideas. Government actions that may unconstitutionally burden this freedom may take many forms, one of which is "intrusion into the internal structure or affairs of an association" like a "regulation that forces the group to accept members it does not desire." Forcing a group to accept certain members may impair the ability of the group to express those views, and only those views, that it intends to express. Thus, "[f]reedom of association . . . plainly presupposes a freedom not to associate."

The forced inclusion of an unwanted person in a group infringes the group's freedom of expressive association if the presence of that person affects in a significant way the group's ability to advocate public or private viewpoints. But the freedom of expressive association, like many freedoms, is not absolute. We have held [in *Roberts*] that the freedom could be overridden "by regulations adopted to serve compelling state interests, unrelated to the suppression of ideas, that cannot be achieved through means significantly less restrictive of associational freedoms."

An Expressive Association

To determine whether a group is protected by the First Amendment's expressive associational right, we must determine whether the group engages in "expressive association." The First Amendment's protection of expressive association is not reserved for advocacy groups. But to come within its ambit, a group must engage in some form of expression, whether it be public or private.... The record reveals the following. The Boy Scouts is a private, nonprofit organization. According to its mission statement:

It is the mission of the Boy Scouts of America to serve others by helping to instill values in young people and, in other ways, to prepare them to make ethical choices over their lifetime in achieving their full potential.

The values we strive to instill are based on those found in the Scout Oath and Law:

Scout Oath

On my honor I will do my best

To do my duty to God and my
country

and to obey the Scout Law;

To help other people at all times;

To keep myself physically strong,

mentally awake, and morally
straight.

Scout Law
A Scout is:
Trustworthy Obedient
Loyal Cheerful
Helpful Thrifty
Friendly Brave
Courteous Clean
Kind Reverent.

Thus, the general mission of the Boy Scouts is clear: "[T]o instill values in young people." The Boy Scouts seeks to instill these values by having its adult leaders spend time with the youth members, instructing and engaging them in activities like camping, archery, and fishing. During the time spent with the youth members, the scoutmasters and assistant scoutmasters inculcate them with the Boy Scouts' values—both expressly and by example. It seems indisputable that an association that seeks to transmit such a system of values engages in expressive activity.

Boy Scouts' View of Homosexuality

Given that the Boy Scouts engages in expressive activity, we must determine whether the forced inclusion of Dale as an assistant scoutmaster would significantly affect the Boy Scouts' ability to advocate public or private viewpoints. This inquiry necessarily requires us first to explore, to a limited extent, the nature of the Boy Scouts' view of homosexuality.

The values the Boy Scouts seeks to instill are "based on" those listed in the Scout Oath and Law. The Boy Scouts explains that the Scout Oath and Law provide "a positive moral code for living; they are a list of 'do's' rather than 'don'ts.'" The Boy Scouts asserts that homosexual conduct is inconsistent with the values embodied in the Scout Oath and Law, particularly with the values represented by the terms "morally straight" and "clean." . . .

A position statement promulgated by the Boy Scouts in 1991 (after Dale's membership was revoked but before this litigation was filed) also supports its current view:

> "We believe that homosexual conduct is inconsistent with the requirement in the Scout Oath that a Scout be morally straight and in the Scout Law that a Scout be clean in word and deed, and that homosexuals do not provide a desirable role model for Scouts."

Interfering with the Boy Scouts' Mission

We must then determine whether Dale's presence as an assistant scoutmaster would significantly burden the Boy Scouts' desire to not "promote homosexual conduct as a legitimate form of behavior." As we give deference to an association's assertions regarding the nature of its expression, we must also give deference to an association's view of what would impair its expression. . . . That is not to say that an expressive association can erect a shield against antidiscrimination laws simply by asserting that mere acceptance of a member from a particular group would impair its message. But here Dale, by his own admission, is one of a group of gay Scouts who have "become leaders in their community and are open and honest about their sexual orientation." Dale was the copresident of a gay and lesbian organization at college and remains a gay rights activist. Dale's presence in the Boy Scouts would, at the very least, force the organization to send a message, both to the youth members and the world, that the Boy Scouts accepts homosexual conduct as a legitimate form of behavior. . . .

Here, we have found that the Boy Scouts believes that homosexual conduct is inconsistent with the values it seeks to instill in its youth members; it will not "promote homosexual conduct as a legitimate form of behavior." . . . The presence of Dale as an assistant scoutmaster would . . . surely interfere with the Boy Scouts' choice not to propound a point of view contrary to its beliefs.

The New Jersey Supreme Court determined that the Boy Scouts' ability to disseminate its message was not significantly affected by the forced inclusion of Dale as an assistant scoutmaster because of the following findings:

> Boy Scout members do not associate for the purpose of disseminating the belief that homosexuality is immoral; Boy Scouts discourages its leaders from disseminating *any* views on sexual issues; and Boy Scouts includes sponsors and members who subscribe to different views in respect of homosexuality.

We disagree with the New Jersey Supreme Court's conclusion drawn from these findings.

Various Objections Answered

First, associations do not have to associate for the "purpose" of disseminating a certain message in order to be entitled to the protections of the First Amendment. An association must merely engage in expressive activity that could be impaired in order to be entitled to protection. . . .

Second, even if the Boy Scouts discourages Scout leaders from disseminating views on sexual issues—a fact that the Boy Scouts disputes with contrary evidence—the First Amendment protects the Boy Scouts' method of expression. If the Boy Scouts wishes Scout leaders to avoid questions of sexuality and teach only by example, this fact does not negate the sincerity of its belief discussed above.

Third, the First Amendment simply does not require that every member of a group agree on every issue in order for the group's policy to be "expressive association." The Boy Scouts takes an official position with respect to homosexual conduct, and that is sufficient for First Amendment purposes. In this same vein, Dale makes much of the claim that the Boy Scouts does not revoke the membership of heterosexual Scout leaders that openly disagree with the Boy Scouts' policy on sexual orientation. But if this is true, it is irrelevant. The presence of an avowed homosexual and gay rights activist in an assistant scoutmaster's uniform sends a distinctly different message from the presence of a heterosexual assistant scoutmaster who is on record as disagreeing with Boy Scouts policy. The Boy Scouts has a First Amendment right to choose to send one message but not the other. The fact that the organization does not trumpet its views from the housetops, or that it tolerates dissent within its ranks, does not mean that its views receive no First Amendment protection. . . .

Where Discrimination Is Not Permitted

We recognized in cases such as *Roberts* and [*Board of Directors of Rotary Int'l v. Rotary Club of*] *Duarte* that States have a compelling interest in eliminating discrimination against women in public accommodations. But in each of these cases we went on to conclude that the enforcement of these statutes would not materially interfere with the ideas that the organization sought to express. In *Roberts*, we said "[i]ndeed, the Jaycees has failed to demonstrate . . . any serious burden on the male members' freedom of expressive association." In *Duarte*, we said:

> [I]mpediments to the exercise of one's right to choose one's associates can violate the right of association protected by the First Amendment. In this case, however, the evidence fails to demonstrate that admitting women to Rotary Clubs will affect in any significant way the existing members' ability to carry out their various purposes.

We thereupon concluded in each of these cases that the organizations' First Amendment rights were not violated by the application of the States' public accommodations laws. . . .

Answering Justice Stevens' Dissent

Justice [John Paul] Stevens' dissent makes much of its observation that the public perception of homosexuality in this country has changed. Indeed, it appears that homosexuality has gained greater societal acceptance. But this is scarcely an argument for denying First Amendment protection to those who refuse to accept these views. The First Amendment protects expression, be it of the popular variety or not. . . . And the fact that an idea may be embraced and advocated by increasing numbers of people is all the more reason to protect the First Amendment rights of those who wish to voice a different view.

Justice Stevens' extolling of Justice [Louis] Brandeis' comments in *New State Ice Co. v. Liebmann* (1932) (dissenting opinion) confuses two entirely different principles. In *New State Ice*, the Court struck down an Oklahoma regulation prohibiting the manufacture, sale, and distribution of ice without a license. Justice Brandeis, a champion of state experimentation in the economic realm, dissented. But Justice Brandeis was never a champion of state experimentation in the suppression of free speech. To the contrary, his First Amendment commentary provides compelling support for the Court's opinion in this case. In speaking of the Founders of this Nation, Justice Brandeis emphasized that they "believed that the freedom to think as you will and to speak as you think are means indispensable to the discovery and spread of political truth." *Whitney v. California*, (concurring opinion). He continued:

> Believing in the power of reason as applied through public discussion, they eschewed silence coerced by law—the argument of force in its worst form. Recognizing the occasional tyrannies of governing majorities, they amended the Constitution so that free speech and assembly should be guaranteed.

Governmental Interference Is Unjustified

We are not, as we must not be, guided by our views of whether the Boy Scouts' teachings with respect to homosexual conduct are right or wrong; public or judicial disapproval of a tenet of an organization's expression does not justify the State's effort to compel the organization to accept members where such acceptance would derogate from the organization's expressive message. "While the law is free to promote all sorts of conduct in place of harmful behavior, it is not free to interfere with speech for no better reason than promoting an approved message or discouraging a disfavored one, however enlightened either purpose may strike the government." [*Hurley*]

The judgment of the New Jersey Supreme Court is reversed, and the cause remanded for further proceedings not inconsistent with this opinion.

The Bill of Rights

CHAPTER 3

The Role of Assembly and Petition in Social Movements

Abolitionists and the Right to Petition

William Lee Miller

From the beginning of the Republic, many Americans were uncomfortable with slavery, but true abolitionists were unpopular and often dismissed as fanatical troublemakers threatening the very existence of the young United States. Still, they had the same right to petition as all Americans, and in the 1800s they began to flood Congress with petitions to outlaw slavery within the nation's capital.

As historian William Lee Miller explains in the excerpt below, the House of Representatives had routine procedures for receiving unpopular petitions that fulfilled their constitutional duties but allowed its members to ignore the grievances themselves. By 1835, however, a number of Southern members were exasperated by these "attacks" on their way of life. When a congressman from Maine introduced one such petition, emphasizing that he himself did not agree with its contents, Representative James Henry Hammond took the unprecedented step of asking that Congress reject the petition altogether. This set off a heated debate on the right to petition that invariably turned into a debate on the very issue that Southerners were trying so hard to suppress: slavery.

Formerly the Thomas C. Sorenson Professor of Political and Social Thought at the University of Virginia, Miller is currently Scholar in Ethics and Institutions at the university's Miller Center of Public Affairs (named for philanthropist Burkett Miller). In addition to Miller's book Arguing About Slavery, *his works on the interplay of politics and morality include* The Business of May Next: James Madison and the Founding *and* Lincoln's Virtues: An Ethical Biography.

William Lee Miller, *Arguing About Slavery: John Quincy Adams and the Great Battle in the United States Congress*, Vintage Books, 1998. © 1995 by William Lee Miller. Used in the U.S., Canada, P.I., Open Market, and E.E.C. by permission of Alfred A. Knopf, a division of Random House, Inc. In the U.K., by permission of the author conveyed by Curtis Brown Ltd.

On December 16, 1835, an otherwise undistinguished thirty-eight-year-old congressman named John Fairfield, from York County, Maine, rose upon his legs in the United States House of Representatives to present the first of that session's petitions for the abolition of slavery in the District of Columbia. He was one of the 242 congressmen from the twenty-four states then in the Union. . . .

This first session of the Twenty-fourth Congress—beginning, as sessions then did, in early December—had just started on December 7. While tardy members were gradually making their way to the capital city, the House had chosen its speaker, adopted its rules, appointed its official printer, filled its committees, and bickered over whether congressmen should be allowed to wear hats in the chamber. December 16 was the first day anything noteworthy happened.

According to House rules, the first thirty days of a congressional session were all petition days. Each day's proceedings started off, after an interlude, with the people's representatives hearing what the people wanted to intercede and remonstrate about. Thereafter, as the House got down to business, only every other Monday was a petition day.

Several of the other congressmen, especially from Massachusetts and Vermont and Pennsylvania, were waiting with petitions upon their desks similar to the one Fairfield had in his hand. Fairfield was the first to present such a petition not from any uniqueness in the particular petition he brought forward, nor from any particular eagerness on his part, but rather by the accident of geography and of House procedure. On petition days the clerk would call the roll of the states not in alphabetical order but, by the quaint early House practice, in a geographical order, starting in the North with the state of Maine. And when his state was called, a congressman would rise to present such petitions and resolutions as he wanted to, or felt he had to. So in December of 1835 Maine was called, and it fell to Mr. Fairfield unintentionally to initiate one of the extraordinary passages in the annals of American government.

Introducing a petition did not mean that one necessarily agreed with the petition's point, any more than one necessarily agreed with a speaker or a newspaper whose guaranteed freedom one affirmed. Congressman Fairfield was careful to explain that he did not himself concur in the "prayer" of this petition he presented; he was simply doing his duty for the 172 ladies in his district who had signed it and sent it to him.

The "Achilles' Heel of Slavery"

A petition asking for the end of slavery in the District of Columbia was nothing new, and not particularly rare. The House had been sporadically receiving petitions for an end to slavery and/or the slave trade since the First Congress, which received such a petition from a group of Philadelphia Quakers. After the establishment of the new federal city in 1800, antislavery petitions had begun to concentrate on the presence of slavery and slave trading in the nation's newly built capital city. Slavery in the District not only was particularly offensive to opponents of slavery, but could not be so plausibly defended by its supporters, who in this case could not invoke states' rights or the original constitutional agreements; the District was not a state, and had not existed when the Constitution was written. Slavery in the District was said, by the classically educated petitioners, to be the Achilles' heel of slavery in the nation. Defending slavery in the District was correspondingly said, by the great opponent of these petitions, [Senator] John C. Calhoun, who was also classically educated, to be the Thermopylae[1] of Southern civilization.

On this December afternoon, however, the nation's representatives, generally speaking, displayed no eagerness either to

1. The narrow pass where three hundred Spartans held off thousands of Persian invaders in 480 B.C.

attack slavery at its Achilles' heel or to defend Southern civilization at its Thermopylae. . . .

The usual practice with petitions on this touchy subject (and often with petitions on other matters as well) had been respectfully to receive them, respectfully to print them, respectfully to assign them to an appropriate committee, and respectfully to allow them to slide thereafter unnoticed into oblivion. Sometimes Congress had been so respectful as to give the abolitionist petitions an answer (invariably the answer, of course, was no). But in the winter of 1835–36 all of this respectfulness was about to wear out.

This was to be the moment, the disinclination of most congressmen and much of the public notwithstanding, when at last the nation's complicated legacy on the subject of African slavery was to force itself into the nation's major forum. The House by its nature could not insulate itself from the currents of public feeling, and the currents on the subject of slavery were now about to become, in some circles, intense.

The more potent intensity in the House was not, as one might expect looking back from the twentieth century, that of the new abolitionists; though they were passionate, they were not powerful, and they were almost nonexistent in the House. The potent new intensity was that of militant slaveholders; their militancy was grounded in what a journalist of the time, Duff Green, called a "morbid sensitivity" that had been provoked by a series of recent events. . . .

The Harbinger of Great Events

Congressman Fairfield, unwittingly holding in his hand the harbinger of great events, moved that the petition from the 172 women in Maine be referred to the Committee on the District of Columbia. That was the routine. That had been the usual action, back in those days of respectfulness; it would have started the petition, as many before it, on its quiet trip to oblivion. But some in the House now wanted a swifter, surer, and less respectful trip. Congressman Cramer, a Democrat from ... New York, moved that the petition be laid on the table—that familiar parliamentary device, not debatable, that abruptly stops debate and if successful puts the motion onto that much overloaded and very metaphorical table, from which it probably—certainly in this case—will never return. Tabling the petition would prevent its being referred to a committee, which had always been a little dangerous; in transit through the House's procedures a petition might leak some discussion of its subject out upon the floor. Now that possibility was to be sealed off. And the House did decide, by a voice vote, to table Mr. Fairfield's petition. So much for the 172 ladies from Maine.

Congressman Fairfield, still doing his duty for his constituents, then presented another petition of the same kind, this time from the same number—172—of gentlemen praying for the same thing: abolition of slavery in the District. No doubt sensing, from the previous action, the mood of the House, this time Fairfield himself moved that the petition be laid on the table. John Y. Mason of Virginia, presumably desiring to make clear the mood of the House, and perhaps also to identify the villains who could pay the slightest attention to such a petition, called for a count of the yeas and nays, which was ordered, and the House then voted by the lopsided vote of 180–31 to "lay the memorial on the table." No discussion. No reference to committee. No response to the petition. The desire to treat these petitions with a more vigorous repudiation than hitherto was clearly gathering strength, and winning victories.

But another viewpoint was also, if not gathering strength, at least showing a new persistence. Congressman William Slade of Vermont, who was one of the very few among the 242 congressmen then in the House who might be suspected of having some actual sympathy with these petitions, moved that this one, despite its tabling, be printed. He argued that if the petitioners were like others whom he knew personally, then they were very respectable people, and not members of "the Abolition society," and that "they were entitled, as a matter of common courtesy to a respectable hearing," and moreover, as "a matter of common right, as well as of common courtesy," that their petition should be printed for the information of members of the House.

But the House was not interested in that information, and not disposed to that courtesy. Another Democrat from New York, a leader of the House named Aaron Vanderpoel, a friend and colleague of the party's new leader, Vice-President [Martin] Van Buren, remarked that this discussion was quite unprofitable—a sentiment that would be echoed many times in the sessions to come—and insisted that House members already knew all they needed to know about what was in these petitions. He therefore moved that the motion to print also be laid on the table, and his motion passed by another overwhelming vote, 168–50. So it was further decided: no printing. The petition, promptly laid on the table without discussion, reference to committee, or response, was not even to be made available to those who wanted to read it. That would seem to have been enough to satisfy even the most ardent opponent of these petitions, and to seal off the subject, and to provide the method for vaporizing any subsequent petitions of the same kind. But given the feelings in some Southern breasts, even this was not enough.

A Surprising Proposal

And given the feeling in a few Northern breasts, those overwhelming negative votes were not enough to stop the presentation of further petitions. Two days later, after the roll call of the states had reached Massachusetts, Congressman William Jackson of that state offered yet another. Such persistence in what the excitable young South Carolinian James Henry Hammond regarded as fanaticism provoked from him a motion that lifted the parliamentary conflict another step above a mere skirmish to the higher plane of major parliamentary warfare. He moved that Jackson's petition *not be received.* Later he altered the wording of his motion to say that the petition be *rejected.* That was a new idea, and set off a month of fireworks. Or nine years of fireworks.

Hammond's stunning remarks on this portentous occasion (Friday, December 18) were reported as follows in the *Congressional Globe* [later known as the *Congressional Record*]:

> *Mr. Hammond* moved that the petition be not received. The large majority by which the House had rejected a similar petition [Mr. Fairfield's] a few days ago had been very gratifying to the whole South. He had hoped it would satisfy the gentlemen charged with such petitions, of the impropriety of introducing them here. Since, however, it had not had that effect, and they persisted still in urging them upon the House and upon the country, he thought it was not requiring too much of the House, to ask it to put a more decided seal of reprobation on them, by peremptorily rejecting this [one].

The Speaker of the House, the future president of the United States, James K. Polk of Tennessee, perhaps a little disconcerted, explained that there was no precedent for such an action as *that*—that a petition, duly presented by a member, not even be *received.* There were various ways a petition could be answered in the negative, or allowed to slip by in silence, but to vote explicitly not to *receive* it—in effect to throw it back indignantly in the face of the petitioners—that was new.

Mr. Hammond, however, had a reason for his motion:

> *Mr. Hammond* . . . did think it due to the House and the country, to give at once the most decisive evidence of the sentiments entertained here upon this subject. He wished to put an end to these petitions. He could not sit there and submit to their being brought forward until the House had

become callous to their consequences. He could not sit there and see the rights of the Southern People assaulted day after day, by the ignorant fanatics from whom these memorials proceed[ed]. . . .

The Case for Rejection

Calhoun and Hammond did have rational arguments for their position—arguments that could be stated in the quiet tones of civic discourse. They held that for Congress to reject the petition was not to infringe the petitioners' right, protected in the First Amendment, because the petitioners had assembled, and written their petition, and had sent it to the congressional bodies, and that therefore their right to petition had in no way been restricted. But, said Calhoun and Hammond, Congress had every right to decide what to do with the petition. It had no obligation to receive it; peremptorily rejecting a petition outright was one of the alternative ways that parliamentary bodies might choose to respond.

And, they said, these particular petitions should be rejected for the soundest of reasons. Congress had no constitutional right to abolish slavery in the District, or for that matter even to discuss slavery anywhere, and therefore Congress should summarily reject petitions on that subject. Their prayer lay outside the powers of Congress. The petitioners were, one might say, like parched farmers petitioning for rain; they were asking for something Congress had no power to grant.

A Troublesome Assertion

But this assertion about Congress's alleged lack of power was troublesome to many. . . . That there was no constitutional right to touch slavery in the original *states* was generally agreed, even by antislavery forces, and there were the specific provisions and compromises in the Constitution that gave that agreement a plausible foundation. But the District? The District of Columbia had not even existed when the Constitution was written. It was the federal city, the city of all the states and all the citizens, of Massachusetts and Maine as much as of South Carolina and Georgia. Moreover, the Constitution did specifically provide, in Article I, Section 8, Paragraph 17, that "[Congress shall have the power to] exercise exclusive legislation in all cases whatsoever over such district (not exceeding ten miles square) as may, by cession of particular states and the acceptance of Congress, become the seat of the Government of the United States."

Why would the framers have used that sweeping phrase "in all cases whatsoever" unless they meant it? Hammond and Calhoun and the most overheated Southerners had an uphill case with that one, and their support dropped off. Almost nobody in Congress proposed actually to *do* anything about slavery in the District, despite all the petitions; but to deny that Congress had the constitutional power to touch slavery in the District if it should choose to—that went too far. It raised the question of whether we were a union after all. . . .

Objections

Even some who were very strongly against abolition—as almost all congressmen were—nevertheless had reservations about this proposed new way of treating the petitions, as an insult to be thrown back in the face of petitioners. There might be a constitutional issue in such a course of action. There certainly could be what later generations would call a public relations problem. Mingled in the speeches of congressmen that winter with the many and varied denunciations of the abolitionist fanatics (almost nobody spoke in their defense), there was an uneasy discussion about the "sacred" right of petition. Caleb Cushing, a distinguished new congressman from Massachusetts, would explain in a learned historical review that the right went back to the Magna Carta; was, after all, guaranteed by the First Amendment to the United States Constitution, and by many state bills of rights as well; was part of the bundle of civil liberties that *defined* the new republic. One could argue that any of the other ways of dealing with petitions—except perhaps laying them on the table without discussion—was sufficient to respect that sacred right, even if nothing whatever was done in response to the petition respectfully referred to committee. But throwing the petition back in the petitioners' faces stamped *rejected*—surely that was not a proper response to the exercise of a sacred right. (Of course, Hammond and Calhoun made clear that they *wanted* the treatment to be disrespectful; that was exactly the point, to show these ignorant fanatics that their petitions were an *insult* to the *honor* of the South, and to make them stop.)

At least many congressmen were uneasy about Hammond's motion—enough to prevent its passage. The earlier, already extreme device of whisking Congressman Jackson's petition into the oblivion of the table—which had seemed extreme enough just two days before, but which was now reduced to comparative moderation by Hammond's (or Calhoun's) superextreme alternative—could not be passed, either. The House got itself into one of those tangles to which parliamentary bodies are subject, in which competing efforts to save time actually waste it, and competing efforts to straighten things out actually produce more snarls. By now one, now another, now a third congressman insisting that no one wanted to talk about the subject of slavery—they talked about it. . . .

An Embarrassing Discovery

There were old motions, new motions, motions to put on the table, rulings by the chair, appeals from rulings by the chair, points of order, calls for the previous question, and inquiries as to just what question was before the House. Such was the parliamentary confusion that the strict South Carolina spokesmen were embarrassed to discover that a petition essentially like those against which they had been so valiantly fighting had already been successfully introduced by Congressman George Briggs of Massachusetts—Jackson had not been the first congressman to rise when Massachusetts had been called—and had absentmindedly been referred, in the heretofore routine procedure of the House, to the Committee on the District of Columbia. . . .

Young Congressman Hammond, on making this disconcerting discovery, sprang to his feet to say that had he known he would have moved to reject Briggs's petition, too.

But parliamentarily speaking, it was now too late for that. What to do? It was decided to make an effort—in a revealing perfectionism that reflected their intensity—to recover Briggs's petition so that it could be more satisfyingly strangled by one of the new methods. But in order to silence it properly it was necessary to get the thing back before the House—to reconsider it. By trying thus to go back and perfect their silencing of every single one of the abolitionist petitions, the more extreme Southern spokesmen shot themselves in the foot, as indeed they would do repeatedly throughout the controversy's nine-year life. The discussion of slavery that flowed on through December 1835 had as its parliamentary foundation the motion to reconsider the referral of Congressman Briggs's petition to committee. Moving to *reconsider* the referral of the Briggs petition to committee opened the floor to exactly that discussion of slavery they had been endeavoring to prevent.

The Women's Movement and the Right to Assemble

Linda J. Lumsden

For many early Americans, the phrase "all men are created equal" was taken literally. Women were held to be distinctly second-class citizens and generally were expected to restrict their activities to the home or possibly the family business. This situation changed in the nineteenth century as many women entered the public arena on behalf of such causes as the abolition of slavery; the temperance movement against alcohol consumption; and eventually the effort to secure suffrage, or the right to vote, for women. As historian Linda J. Lumsden reveals in the following selection, the right of peaceable assembly was a vital component at every step of the way.

By speaking publicly and organizing mass demonstrations in their effort to abolish slavery and outlaw alcohol, activist women proved that they and many other women were interested in the vital issues of the day. Drawing on these experiences, women first secured the right to vote and went on to organize on behalf of equal rights for women throughout society. These movements often met with great opposition, including hostility from governmental officials, but the women who participated in them had the First Amendment on their side. Again and again, by asserting their constitutional right of assembly, women fundamentally altered age-old cultural assumptions about their proper role and launched a women's rights movement that continues to this day.

An assistant professor of journalism at Western Kentucky University, Lumsden is also a historian of the women's rights movement and the author of Inez: The Life and Times of Inez Milholland, *the biography of a prominent suffragist and activist on behalf of women workers and the reform of divorce laws.*

The suffrage movement exemplified how the right of assembly can effect change in a democracy. Arguably the most ancient and basic principle of a free society, the right of assembly served suffragists well during the 1910s. As a disfranchised class with limited resources, suffragists took their message to the streets—that most public and accessible forum—forced their ideas upon an indifferent public, and gradually won over a significant portion of the public and politicians, who also were besieged by suffrage assemblies in male political bodies. Suffrage only became a national issue when women publicly agitated for the vote. If they had not taken to the streets—to soapbox, solicit petitions, parade, or picket—the suffrage movement never would have gotten off the ground, because no one was eager to listen to suffragists' ideas, much less act upon them. The right of assembly provided the foundation for every step of the suffrage campaign.

Suffragists also challenged beliefs about how women should behave when they took to the streets to speak, march, and picket.... Among the minorities that fought for freedom of expression by staging a broad range of demonstrations during the tumultuous decade that encompassed World War I, suffragists indirectly helped prod the legal system to establish protections for dissidents exercising their First Amendment rights.

The Importance of the Right of Assembly

The right of assembly protects people meeting together or the communication of ideas among people to accomplish various common purposes. It is the foundation for all other forms of freedom of expression, because ideas must be shared before they can have an impact upon society. "The important political right of assembly and petition is rather the original than a derivation from freedom of speech," explained constitutional law scholar Frederic Jesup Stimson in 1908. According to a pair of later legal scholars [James Jarrett and Vernon Mund],

"An assembly of two or more people is a necessary basis for the exercise of the right of freedom of speech and a multitude of other privileges." . . .

The role of outdoor meetings in self-governance has been respected by free societies throughout history. "Wherever the title of streets and parks may rest, they have immemorially been held in trust for the use of the public and, time out of mind, have been used for purposes of assembly, communicating thought between citizens," asserted the United States Supreme Court in [*Hague v. CIO,*] a landmark case involving the right of assembly. The leading nineteenth-century Court case on the right of assembly [*U.S. v. Cruikshank*] simply stated: "It is found wherever civilization exists." The concept of a right of assembly was first set down on paper in 1215 in the Magna Carta, from which all Anglo-Saxon civil liberties flow. . . .

Assemblies Restricted in Early America

Because of the disruptive potential of street assemblies, the Bill of Right's rhetorical homage to the right of assembly was not matched by legal protections for assemblies. For one thing, the First Amendment was not considered applicable to state laws prior to 1925. Courts ruled erratically on all First Amendment freedoms until well into the twentieth century and were especially hostile to gatherings of politically radical groups. Prior to the 1920s, the United States Supreme Court with one minor exception ruled against the few free-speech defenses it heard. It would take the courts half a century to catch up with pioneering legal scholar Thomas Cooley's declaration in 1868 that freedom of expression was "essential to the very existence and perpetuity of free government."

Courts seldom considered First Amendment issues prior to the late nineteenth century. From 1791 to 1889, the United States Supreme Court heard only twelve cases involving speech and press issues. Between 1890 and 1917, the Court heard fifty-three such cases, still an average of just two a year. Partly because of its unfamiliarity with free-speech issues, "the Court's opinions often were illogical or inconsistent," noted legal historian Michael Gibson. Most nineteenth-century First Amendment cases never even went to court, partly because of extrajudicial factors such as threats of violence and economic and social pressures. And greater emphasis was placed upon the police power to protect the public's health, safety, and morals. . . .

Women Denied the Right of Assembly

Given the chilly reception nineteenth-century courts accorded freedom of expression, it probably was lucky for women that courts addressed no cases involving women and freedom of expression in the nineteenth century. The main reason for the absence of such cases, however, was that extralegal cultural proscriptions denied women the right of assembly among other constitutional rights. In eighteenth-century America, freedom of expression was linked to politics, and politics belonged in the public sphere, which remained taboo for women. Women had to fight to assert their right to assemble peaceably. "If today women can be said to have obtained freedom of expression in the United States," noted colonial historian Mary Beth Norton, "they have achieved that goal through their own efforts, not because a 'great man' of the past sought to extend them the right of free speech."

The Founding Fathers spoke literally when they declared all men are created equal. Women lacked basic civil rights, such as the vote, control over their property and wages, custodianship of their children, and access to the professions and education. They were confined to duties in the home, whereas men controlled politics. . . .

Abolitionism and Women's Rights

The abolition movement proved the crucible for women who dared speak their minds. The key role abolition played in cre-

Women carry ballot boxes promoting women's suffrage in 1917. In early America, women were considered second-class citizens, and the right to vote came about as a direct result of their ability to engage in public agitation and protest. © Bettmann/Corbis

ating the woman's rights movement is undebatable. "As abolitionists they first won their right to speak in public, and began to evolve a philosophy of their place in society and of their basic rights," said suffrage historian Eleanor Flexner. Abolition also honed women's experience in wielding the right to petition, which would figure prominently in the twentieth-century suffrage movement.

Lucy Stone, the nation's first full-time woman's rights speaker, was just one leader who emerged from the abolition movement. At times she was peppered with coins, dried apples, fish, beans, tobacco, and even a hymnal hurled so hard it stunned her. When Abby Kelley launched her antislavery lectures in 1838, she endured slurs such as "nigger bitch," "man woman," "Jezebel," and "infidel." "During two decades of public speaking she dodged rotten eggs, rum bottles, and the contents of outhouses," wrote her biographer [Dorothy Sterling]. "The appearances of the antislavery women on the platform were praised as angelic and excoriated as diabolical," concluded historian Jean Fagan Yellin, "but in and through their public presence they dramatized the possibility of female freedom on a human level."

Because women abolitionists had to fight to meet and speak, freedom of assembly and freedom of speech were indelibly linked with the women's rights movement from its genesis in the abolition movement. Nineteenth-century woman's rights activists recognized the link between their second-class status and their inability to speak up for themselves. "Woman is taught to refrain from any public expression of speech or intellect, from a religious principle, as a tribute of adulation to man's superiority," Paulina Davis told the first national woman's rights convention in 1850. Women's experiences on the abolition trail vividly demonstrated to them the connection between the freedom to assemble and to speak with other civil rights.

The Fight to Speak

Trailblazers in the fight for women to speak and meet freely were South Carolina abolitionists Sarah and Angelina Grimké. Angelina Grimké's words in the 1830s on the link between slavery and women's status sowed the seeds for nineteenth-century feminism. She defined freedom as engagement in significant action and characterized significant action as public speech. In other words, she recognized that free speech was a precondition for women to be free. She wrote, "If we have no right to act, then may we well be termed 'the white slaves of the North'—for, like our brethren in bonds, we must seal our lips in silence and despair."

Numerous encroachments upon the Grimké sisters' right to meet and speak characterized their antislavery speaking tour before "promiscuous audiences" (containing men and women) across Massachusetts in 1837. Officials often denied them meeting places. Critics called them names. The venom spewed at the Grimkés and the women who followed them was part of a larger public antipathy toward the abolitionist movement that sparked an assault upon fundamental American values such as free speech, a free press, and the right to assemble peaceably.

In the Grimkés' case, a Massachusetts newspaper editor not only censored Angelina's speech, part of the first public debate between a man and a woman, but Congregational pastors wrote a letter to their congregations condemning the Grimkés for violating New Testament injunctions against women participating in public life. Sarah Grimké responded in a series of landmark articles in which she asserted that the Bible merely reflected the patriarchal society that produced it. "I ask no favors for my sex," she wrote. "All I ask our brethren is, that they will take their feet from off our necks, and permit us to stand upright on that ground which God designed us to occupy." Her sister also replied, saying: "If we surrender the right to *speak* in public this year, we must surrender the right to petition the next year, and the right to *write* the year after, and so on. What *then* can *woman* do for the slave, when she is herself under the feet of man and shamed into *silence*?"

First Woman's Rights Convention

Abolition provided the impetus for the first woman's rights convention, in fact, when the World's Anti-Slavery Convention in London in 1840—presumably comprising the planet's most egalitarian-minded men—forced eight American women delegates to sit behind a curtain in a gallery and forbade them to speak. The injustice and indignity spurred Lucretia Mott and Elizabeth Cady Stanton to organize the Woman's Rights Convention in Seneca Falls, New York, on 19–20 July 1848. From that moment, woman's rights conventions, predicated upon the right to assemble peaceably, formed the core of the woman's rights movement.

Unfamiliar with how to run a convention, the women perused male productions. "The reports of Peace, Temperance, and Anti-Slavery conventions were examined, but all alike seemed too tame and pacific for the inauguration of a rebellion such as the world had never before seen," recorded the *History of Woman Suffrage.* Finally, they adopted the Declaration of Independence as the model for their Declaration of Sentiments seeking improved property and child custody rights, better professional and educational opportunities, and the most radical demand—the vote.

A New Kind of Power

Why so radical? As historian Ellen DuBois observed, feminists' focus on citizenship called for a new kind of power for women not based in the family; a nonfamilial role for women in the public sphere challenged the male monopoly on the public arena. "This," wrote DuBois, "is what gave suffragism much of its feminist meaning."

This helps explain why men found woman suffrage so threatening. The vote symbolized female autonomy. It threatened the social order, because full citizenship for women implied a revolutionary change in the conception of woman. The vote also implied parallel changes in men's role, which helps explain why so many antisuffrage articles and cartoons caricatured men pushing baby carriages, washing dishes, or performing other female tasks. The idea of women imposing their morality and values upon the male political system caused many cigar-chomping, whiskey-swilling, epithet-spewing backroom politicos to eye them as a "Puritan scourge incarnate." But men were not the only Americans unsettled by the idea; most women also opposed suffrage and the changes it portended for women's well-defined role.

Why did a handful of women so covet the vote that they defied such well-entrenched legal and cultural authority? The ballot conferred citizenship upon its holder, and citizenship conferred humanity. As suffrage historian Eleanor Flexner wrote, the vote represented for women "a vital step toward winning human dignity, and the recognition that they too were endowed with the faculty of reason, the power of judgment, the capacity for social responsibility." The symbolism was so tied up with humanity that innumerable suffrage talks and essays sought to answer the question "Are Women Human Beings?"

A Radical Course

The women assembling in Seneca Falls had embarked upon a radical course. The mere act of women assembling on their own behalf without cover of offering charity or studying meekly to improve their mothering was so radical that even the bold convention organizers shrank from leading discussions. James Mott chaired the Woman's Rights Convention. "The proceedings were extensively published, unsparingly ridiculed by the press and denounced by the pulpit," the *History of Woman Suffrage* recorded. The ridicule prompted women to vigorously exercise their right to a free press by launching several suffrage newspapers, another important First Amendment tool of the woman's rights movement.

The right of assembly figured prominently as women convened in Ohio, Indiana, Pennsylvania, and Massachusetts. The first National Woman's Rights Convention in Worcester, Massachusetts, on 23–24 October 1850, attracted a thousand persons from as far away as California. Women soon gained the confidence to run their own rights conventions. "Not a man was allowed to sit on the platform, to speak, or vote," the *History of Woman Suffrage* recorded of a convention in Salem, Ohio. "*Never did men so suffer.*"

The radical nature of woman's rights conventions occasionally prompted the abrogation of their rights of assembly. Ohio women were denied use of the local school and church for a rights convention. The women found shelter on the threshing floor of a barn filled with more than three hundred farm families.

Harassment and Ridicule

Men also employed harassment and ridicule to abort women's public gatherings. Hecklers turned an 1853 woman's rights convention into a riot at the Broadway Tabernacle in New York. "Gentlemen and ladies alike who attempted to speak were interrupted by shouts, hisses, stamping, and cheers, rude remarks, and all manner of noisy demonstrations," the *History of Woman Suffrage* reported. Speaker Wendell Phillips told the crowd, "You prove one thing to-night, that the men of New York do not understand the meaning of civil liberty and free discussion." The uproar forced the convention to close.

Instead of criticizing the disruptive audience, the *New York Herald* ridiculed the women, a typical press reaction to woman's rights assemblies. "The assemblage of rampant women which convened at the Tabernacle yesterday was an interesting phase in the comic history of the nineteenth century," its editorial began, launching into a lampoon of the women's goals. The newspaper used a timeworn tactic for silencing women: questioning their womanhood. It asserted that participants in the "gathering of unsexed women" at the "Women's Wrong Convention" were "entirely devoid of personal attraction." The ridicule was yet another example of the extralegal pressures that stymied women's expression of the right of assembly. Twentieth-century suffragists, however, would proudly appropriate the label "rampant women."

African Americans were among the "rampant women" prominent in the movement in the nineteenth century. They played an integral role in early woman's rights conventions, in contrast to the ostracism by white suffragists they endured after the turn of the century. Stanton's radical resolution calling for woman suffrage at Seneca Falls, for instance, seemed doomed until [black abolitionist and journalist] Frederick Douglass vigorously endorsed it. Suffrage was a joint goal of black and white activists who together created the American Equal Rights Association (AERA) after the Civil War. Nineteenth-century woman's rights assemblies engaged in a dialogue about race and privilege absent from the twentieth-century suffrage movement. Frances E. W. Harper, the black poet, novelist, and civil rights activist, won cheers when she told the AERA: "I do not believe the white women are dew-drops just exhaled from the skies.... You white women speak here of rights. I speak of wrongs. I, as a colored woman, have had in this country an education which has made me feel as if I were in the situation of [biblical patriarch Abraham's son] Ishmael, my hand against every man, and every man's hand against me." ...

Temperance Crusade

Temperance was another nineteenth-century women's movement that profoundly influenced twentieth-century suffragists. The Woman's Temperance Crusade during the winter of 1873–74 was the nation's first women's mass movement, enlisting hundreds of thousands of women in hundreds of towns who marched to liquor outlets to sing and pray in what a historian [Susan Dye Lee] called a "spectacular nineteenth-century version of street theater." The crusade deployed the right of assembly in mass meetings outdoors, parades, and picketing, all new forms of female public protest that swept temperance women into civil disobedience. The crusade truly was militant: Delegations not only prayed on saloon floors and blocked shipments of liquor with picket lines but also occasionally destroyed casks of liquor with hatchets. As historian Ruth Bordin has pointed out, middle-class women excused their indecorous protests by tying their militant movement to the home. They claimed they were protecting the domestic sphere by ridding society of the evils of alcohol. These exercises in civil disobedience also helped awaken women to their entitlement to civil liberties. The cask smashers, for instance, defended their actions with analogies to the Boston Tea Party.

But these experiments in public protest still posed danger. Beer and sausages rained upon temperance protesters in Ohio, and a mob with dogs set upon militant crusaders in Cleveland. Marchers were convicted of disturbing the peace in Portland, Oregon, ordinances aimed at banning the marches were enacted in Cleveland and Cincinnati, and an injunction blocked women from singing and praying in an Ohio beer garden. "The crusaders' marches, undertaken in the face of hostile crowds and violent resistance by liquor dealers and their supporters, represented an attempt to exercise the right to participate in public affairs," noted historian Jack S. Blocker Jr. They succeeded within months in dropping the nation's malt liquor production by five and a half million gallons.

The crusade's true significance was far broader. The mass movement served as "one of the most powerful instruments of women's consciousness-raising of all time," Bordin concluded. Many leaders of the fledgling suffrage movement launched their activism in the Woman's Christian Temperance Union (WCTU), including [Susan B.] Anthony and future NAWSA [National American Woman Suffrage Association] presidents Dr. Anna Howard Shaw and Carrie Chapman Catt. Anthony organized the first state woman's temperance organization in 1852 after the Sons of Temperance banned women from speaking at their convention. In turn, the inaugural convention of the WCTU excluded male members.

Anthony later uncharacteristically objected to temperance protests' "desecration of womanhood," but most female crusaders came away with a new appreciation for the power of assembly and association. The crusade impressed upon women the power of public protest. "It really seems to me that nothing short of the street praying movement will arouse the apathy and indifference among men," wrote one crusader

[Rebecca Janney]. In the twentieth century, a handful of militant suffragists would come to similar conclusions when they defied society to picket the White House in wartime. By the end of the nineteenth century, women had gained considerable expertise and confidence in expressing their demands through the right to assemble peaceably.

Freedom of Assembly Was Crucial to the Civil Rights Movement

David L. Hudson Jr.

The civil rights movement of the 1950s and 1960s was a pri-mary beneficiary of the right of peaceable assembly. As First Amendment Center research lawyer David L. Hudson Jr. makes clear in the following analysis, the marches and demonstrations that ultimately overthrew the system of racial segregation throughout the South depended on the First Amendment right of assembly for their success. In turn, the attempts by state and lo-cal governments to suppress these demonstrations forced the issue into the courts, which consistently found that sit-ins and other protests were constitutionally protected forms of the right to free expression. Indeed, by challenging restrictive laws, civil rights or-ganizations such as the National Association for the Advance-ment of Colored People reinvigorated the right to associate freely, which had lost considerable ground in the anti-Communist hys-teria of the 1940s and 1950s.

The First Amendment played a crucial role in the epic struggles of the civil rights movement of the 1950s and '60s, when Dr. Martin Luther King Jr. and countless others en-gaged in sit-ins, protests, marches and other demonstrations to force social change.

The rights of free speech and assembly enabled civil rights protesters on the streets of Birmingham and Selma, Ala., and other cities throughout the South to force society to improve the treatment of African-Americans.

David L. Hudson Jr., "Assembly: Civil Rights and First Amendment," www.firstamend mentcenter.org. Reproduced by permission.

The Foundation of the Civil Rights Movement

"The First Amendment right of assembly was the foundation of the civil rights movement of the 1950s," said Western Kentucky University journalism professor Linda Lumsden, who has written on the role of freedom of assembly in the women's-suffrage movement.

"The civil rights movement featured various forms of free expression," University of Columbia law professor Jack Greenberg said in an interview in 1999.

Greenberg, who served as the director-counsel of the NAACP [National Association for the Advancement of Colored People] Legal Defense and Educational Fund, Inc. from 1961 until 1984, listed the petition for redress of grievances by students in Columbia, S.C., the march from Selma to Birmingham, the freedom rides, the sit-ins and the demonstrations in Birmingham as prime examples of civil rights advocates engaging in First Amendment–protected activities.

University of Pennsylvania professor Robert Richards, author of *Freedom's Voice: The Perilous Present and Uncertain Future of the First Amendment*, agreed that "the First Amendment was the key tool of the civil rights movement." "Without the First Amendment and the protections breathed into it by the courts, the movement would not have flourished as much as it did," Richards said.

Lumsden said that "the peaceful, nonviolent protesting raised public consciousness, challenged people's beliefs and attacked the forces of power."

"The Supreme Court is influenced by the cultural, political and societal influences of the times," Lumsden said. "It helped the civil rights protesters that their cause was so sympathetic."

The Movement Reinvigorated the First Amendment

Not only was the First Amendment essential to the civil rights movement, but the movement itself also galvanized First

Amendment ideals into legal precedent. In his 1965 book *The Negro and the First Amendment,* legal scholar Harry Kalven foresaw the unique changes in First Amendment law that would grow out of the civil rights movement. In fact, Kalven wrote, "We may come to see the Negro as winning back for us the freedoms the Communists seemed to have lost for us," a reference to civil liberties sacrificed during the anticommunist "red scare" era of the 1950s and early '60s.

First Amendment expert Robert O'Neil, founder of the Thomas Jefferson Center for the Protection of Free Expression, said many areas of First Amendment law were shaped by the civil rights movement. "The sources of pressure created by the civil rights movement coincided at a time when the courts were receptive to the expansion of First Amendment principles," O'Neil said.

A New Understanding of Demonstrators' Rights

The cases that grew out of civil rights–era activism clearly show the force of the First Amendment in persuading the Supreme Court to issue rulings in favor of the demonstrators. "Nearly all the cases involving the civil rights movement were decided on First Amendment grounds," Greenberg said.

Margaret Blanchard, the William Rand Kenan journalism professor at the University of North Carolina [UNC], said that "the civil rights protesters broke new ground in organizing together for certain causes, using various kinds of symbolic expression and emphasizing the right to march."

Blanchard said numerous court decisions across the country sided with civil rights protesters who challenged parade ordinances. The ordinances vested too much power in city officials who could—and sometimes would—deny permits because they disliked the group or its cause.

Supreme Court Cases

The Supreme Court issued several rulings protecting civil rights advocates from criminal charges for engaging in First Amendment–protected activity. In the 1963 decision *Edwards v. South Carolina*, the high court struck down the breach-of-the-peace convictions of 187 African-American students who marched to the South Carolina Statehouse carrying signs with messages such as "Down with Segregation."

Saying the "circumstances in this case reflect an exercise of these basic constitutional rights in their most pristine and classic form," the Court ruled that the government could not criminalize "the peaceful expression of unpopular views."

In its 1961 decision *Garner v. Louisiana*, the court overturned the disturbing-the-peace convictions of five African-Americans who engaged in sit-ins at an all-white café counter in Baton Rouge. In his concurring opinion, Justice John Harlan wrote that a sit-in demonstration "is as much a part of the free trade of ideas as is verbal expression."

Harlan wrote that a sit-in was entitled to the same level of First Amendment protection as "displaying a red flag as a symbol of opposition to organized government," a form of expression that the Supreme Court protected in the 1931 case *Stromberg v. People of California*.

Key NAACP Cases

Numerous other First Amendment–related Supreme Court decisions stemmed from events during the civil rights movement. Among these cases O'Neil lists *NAACP v. Alabama* (1958), which protected the free-association rights of NAACP members from official harassment, and *NAACP v. Button* (1963), which ensured access to courts and protected the associational freedoms of public-interest groups.

In *NAACP v. Alabama*, state officials demanded the names and addresses of all the members of the National Association for the Advancement of Colored People of Alabama. But the

Supreme Court held that compelling the disclosure of membership lists would violate members' First Amendment free-association rights. The high court wrote that "privacy in group association may in many circumstances be indispensable to preservation of freedom of association, particularly where a group espouses dissident beliefs."

UNC's Blanchard said, "*NAACP v. Alabama* established the right of people to join together to advocate causes even in hostile environments."

Five years later, in *NAACP v. Button*, the Supreme Court ruled that the NAACP had the right to refer individuals who wanted to sue in public school desegregation cases to lawyers and to pay their litigation expenses. (This case also relates to the First Amendment freedom of petition. . . .)

A Virginia law had forbidden any organization from compensating an attorney in a case in which it had no direct monetary interest, and also had forbidden organizations from intervening between lawyer and client. State officials charged the NAACP with violating these rules by encouraging people to become plaintiffs in desegregation cases, referring them to private attorneys and then paying their litigation expenses. However, the Supreme Court ruled that the NAACP's actions were "modes of expression and association protected by the First Amendment."

Greenberg called *Button* "extraordinarily important" because it represented the beginning of the public-interest law firm. . . .

Mutual Reenforcement

Each of these cases demonstrates the role that the First Amendment played in the civil rights movement and likewise shows the important role that the civil rights movement played in the development of First Amendment freedoms. "It is likely that the same First Amendment doctrines would not have developed at the same rate and with the same force or conviction were it not for the civil rights movement," O'Neil said.

The Supreme Court in these various rulings strengthened people's right to assemble peaceably—as well as to speak out and petition government—in protest against injustices.

Appendix

The Origins of the American Bill of Rights

The U.S. Constitution as it was originally created and submitted to the colonies for ratification in 1787 did not include what we now call the Bill of Rights. This omission was the cause of much controversy as Americans debated whether to accept the new Constitution and the new federal government it created. One of the main concerns voiced by opponents of the document was that it lacked a detailed listing of guarantees of certain fundamental individual rights. These critics did not succeed in preventing the Constitution's ratification, but were in large part responsible for the existence of the Bill of Rights.

In 1787 the United States consisted of thirteen former British colonies that had been loosely bound since 1781 by the Articles of Confederation. Since declaring their independence from Great Britain in 1776, the former colonies had established their own colonial governments and constitutions, eight of which had bills of rights written into them. One of the most influential was Virginia's Declaration of Rights. Drafted largely by planter and legislator George Mason in 1776, the seventeen-point document combined philosophical declarations of natural rights with specific limitations on the powers of government. It served as a model for other state constitutions.

The sources for these declarations of rights included English law traditions dating back to the 1215 Magna Carta and the 1689 English Bill of Rights—two historic documents that provided specific legal guarantees of the "true, ancient, and indubitable rights and liberties of the people" of England. Other legal sources included the colonies' original charters, which declared that colonists should have the same "privileges, franchises, and immunities" that they would if they lived in England. The ideas concerning natural rights developed by John Locke and other English philosophers were also influential. Some of these concepts of rights had been cited in the Declaration of Independence to justify the American Revolution.

Unlike the state constitutions, the Articles of Confederation, which served as the national constitution from 1781 to 1788, lacked a bill of rights. Because the national government under the Articles of Confederation had little authority by design, most people believed it posed little threat to civil liberties, rendering a bill of rights unnecessary. However, many influential leaders criticized the very weakness of the national government for creating its own problems; it did not create an effective system for conducting a coherent foreign policy, settling disputes between states, printing money, and coping with internal unrest.

It was against this backdrop that American political leaders convened in Philadelphia in May 1787 with the stated intent to amend the Articles of Confederation. Four months later the Philadelphia Convention, going beyond its original mandate, created a whole new Constitution with a stronger national government. But while the new Constitution included a few provisions protecting certain civil liberties, it did not include any language similar to Virginia's Declaration of Rights. Mason, one of the delegates in Philadelphia, refused to sign the document. He listed his objections in an essay that began:

> There is no Declaration of Rights, and the Laws of the general government being paramount to the laws and constitution of the several States, the Declaration of Rights in the separate States are no security.

Mason's essay was one of hundreds of pamphlets and other writings produced as the colonists debated whether to ratify the new Constitution (nine of the thirteen colonies had to officially ratify the Constitution for it to go into effect). The supporters of the newly drafted Constitution became known as Federalists, while the loosely organized group of opponents were called Antifederalists. Antifederalists opposed the new Constitution for several reasons. They believed the presidency would create a monarchy, Congress would not be truly representative of the people, and state governments would be endangered. However, the argument that proved most effective was that the new document lacked a bill of rights and thereby threatened Americans with the loss of cherished individual liberties. Federalists realized that to gain the support of key states such as New York and Virginia, they needed to pledge to offer amendments to the Constitution that would be added immediately after its ratification. Indeed, it was not until this promise was made that the requisite number of colonies ratified the document. Massachusetts, Virginia, South Carolina, New Hampshire, and New York all included amendment recommendations as part of their decisions to ratify.

One of the leading Federalists, James Madison of Virginia, who was elected to the first Congress to convene under the new Constitution, took the lead in drafting the promised amendments. Under the process provided for in the Constitution, amendments needed to be passed by both the Senate and House of Representatives and then ratified by three-fourths of the states. Madison sifted through the suggestions provided by the states and drew upon the Virginia Declaration of Rights and other state documents in composing twelve amendments, which he introduced to Congress in September 1789. "If they are incorporated into the constitution," he argued in a speech introducing his proposed amendments,

> Independent tribunals of justice will consider themselves in
> a peculiar manner the guardians of those rights; they will be
> an impenetrable bulwark against every assumption of power

in the legislative or executive; they will be naturally led to resist every encroachment upon rights expressly stipulated for in the constitution by the declaration of rights.

After debate and some changes to Madison's original proposals, Congress approved the twelve amendments and sent them to the states for ratification. Two amendments were not ratified; the remaining ten became known as the Bill of Rights. Their ratification by the states was completed on December 15, 1791.

Supreme Court Cases Involving the Rights to Peaceable Assembly and to Petition

1876

United States v. Cruikshank

The Court declared the right to peaceable assembly an "attribute of national citizenship" that could not be encroached by the federal government.

1937

De Jonge v. Oregon

The Court ruled that the right to peaceable assembly was as fundamental as the right to free speech and could not be infringed by states and localities.

1939

Hague v. C.I.O.

The Court found that streets and sidewalks are public spaces and using them to air grievances does not constitute "disorderly conduct."

1940

Thornhill v. Alabama

The Court held that orderly picketing by unions cannot be prosecuted as "loitering" and that state laws against picketing are unconstitutional.

1941

Cox v. New Hampshire

The Court upheld license requirements and other restrictions on public demonstrations as long as they are reasonable and truly designed to maintain public order.

1958
NAACP v. Alabama
The Court found that an attempt to force the National Association for the Advancement of Colored People to turn over their membership list amounted to a threat to the organization itself and therefore an unconstitutional attack on the freedom of association.

1961
Scales v. United States
Although membership in a "subversive" organization is constitutional, the Court found that members of an organization that advocates the violent overthrow of the U.S. government can be prosecuted if they knowingly and actively support the organization's subversive activities.

1961
Eastern Railroad Presidents Conference v. Noerr Motor Freight, Inc.
The Court held that corporations that join together to seek overturn of laws or regulations cannot be held liable for antitrust violation, in effect ruling that the right to petition supersedes antitrust legislation.

1963
Edwards v. South Carolina
The Court declared that police and other local authorities cannot use fear of rioting, or the presence of unruly spectators, as an excuse to prevent peaceful demonstrators from exercising their right to assemble and air their grievances.

1965
Cox v. Louisiana
The Court effectively struck down a number of state laws that barred public speakers from advocating actions that had the potential to lead to violence. The Court found these "breach of the peace" provisions too broad and an unconstitutional infringement on free speech and the right to peaceable assembly.

1980

Pruneyard Shopping Center v. Robins

The Court found that states can infringe on the property rights of largely public places to protect the right to petition, as long as regulations are reasonable.

1980

Missouri v. NOW

The Court struck down an attempt to penalize an organization for advocating a boycott that would economically harm a state, finding that any such attempt violates the right to petition government for redress of grievances.

1984

Roberts v. United States Jaycees

States can impose certain restrictions on associations, including banning gender discrimination by organizations that have a large, otherwise open membership and no clearly expressed purpose that would be inconsistent with admitting women to full membership.

1999

Chicago v. Morales

The Court found that a city ordinance allowing police officers to arrest "criminal street gang members" for loitering was too vague and allowed too much discretion to police officers, thus violating both the right to assembly and the Fourteenth Amendment's due process guarantee.

2000

Boy Scouts of America v. James Dale

The Court held that organizations cannot be compelled to accommodate members or groups that violate its clear and public position on an issue.

2002

BE&K Construction Co. v. National Labor Relations Board
The Court specifically affirmed the longstanding notion that the right to petition included a fundamental right to initiate lawsuits.

For Further Research

M. Glenn Abernathy, *The Right of Assembly and Association.* Columbia: University of South Carolina Press, 1981.

American Bar Association, *After City of Chicago v. Jesus Morales: A Resource Guide for Teachers.* Chicago: ABA Division for Public Education, 2000.

Lucy Barber, *Marching on Washington: The Forging of an American Political Tradition.* Berkeley: University of California Press, 2002.

Robert Bresler, *Freedom of Association: Rights and Liberties Under the Law.* Santa Barbara, CA: ABC-CLIO, 2004.

Alexis de Tocqueville, *Democracy in America, Volume I*, translated by Henry Reeve as revised by Francis Bowen. New York: Alfred A. Knopf, 1945.

Joel M. Gora, Gary M. Stern, Mort Halperin, and David Goldberger, *The Right to Protest: The Basic ACLU Guide to Free Expression.* Carbondale: Southern Illinois University Press, 1991.

David Hamlin, *Nazi-Skokie Conflict: A Civil Liberties Battle.* Boston: Beacon Press, 1980.

Thomas R. Hensley, ed., *The Boundaries of Freedom of Expression and Order in American Democracy.* Kent, OH: Kent State University Press, 2001.

Harry Kalven, *The Negro and the First Amendment.* Columbus: Ohio State University Press, 1965.

Philip Klinkner, *The First Amendment.* Englewood Cliffs, NJ: Silver Burdett Press, 1991.

Margaret Kohn, *Brave New Neighborhoods: The Privatization of Public Space.* New York: Routledge, 2004.

James E. Leahy, *The First Amendment, 1791–1991: Two Hundred Years of Freedom.* Jefferson, NC: McFarland & Co., 1991.

Linda J. Lumsden, *Rampant Women: Suffragists and the Right of Assembly.* Knoxville: University of Tennessee Press, 1997.

Harvey C. Mansfield, *Present Dangers: Rediscovering the First Amendment.* Dallas TX: Spence Publishing Co., 2003.

Eugene J. McCarthy, *The Ultimate Tyranny: The Majority over the Majority.* New York: Harcourt Brace Jovanovich, 1980.

Darien A. McWhirter, *Freedom of Speech, Press, and Assembly.* Phoenix, AZ: Oryx Press, 1994.

William Lee Miller, *Arguing about Slavery: John Quincy Adams and the Great Battle in the United States Congress.* New York: Vintage Books, 1998.

Paul L. Murphy, *The Shaping of the First Amendment: 1791 to the Present.* New York: Oxford University Press, 1992.

Samuel P. Nelson, *Beyond the First Amendment: The Politics of Free Speech and Pluralism.* Baltimore, MD: Johns Hopkins University Press, 2005.

Robert D. Richards, *Freedom's Voice: The Perilous Present and Uncertain Future of the First Amendment.* Washington, DC: Brasseys, 1998.

Isidore Starr, *The Idea of Liberty: First Amendment Freedoms.* St. Paul, MN: West Publishing Co., 1978.

Phillipa Strum, *When the Nazis Came to Skokie: Freedom for Speech We Hate.* Lawrence: University Press of Kansas, 1999.

Web Sites

American Civil Liberties Union, Free Speech: Right to Protest, www.aclu.org/freespeech/protest/index.html. This site provides a regularly updated list of important ACLU lawsuits involving the right to protest and related issues of assembly.

FindLaw Constitution Center, www.findlaw.com/casecode/ constitution. A clearinghouse for lawyers, law students, and the public, this site provides links to case law and judicial interpretation of the Constitution and its amendments, including the First Amendment rights of peaceable assembly and petitioning for redress of grievances.

First Amendment Center, http://www.firstamendmentcenter. com. This is the Web site of the Freedom Forum, affiliated with Vanderbilt University. It provides summaries, commentary, and access to numerous books, articles, and programs on First Amendment freedoms, including the rights to peaceable assembly and to petition the government.

Index